# Sports Illustrated
# TUMBLING

# THE SPORTS ILLUSTRATED LIBRARY

BOOKS ON TEAM SPORTS

Baseball
*Basketball

Football: Defense
Football: Offense
Football: Quarterback

Ice Hockey
Pitching
Soccer
Volleyball

BOOKS ON INDIVIDUAL SPORTS

*Bowling
Fly Fishing
*Golf
Handball
Horseback Riding
Judo
*Racquetball
*Running for Women

Skiing
Squash
Table Tennis
*Tennis
Track: Running Events
Track: Field Events
Wrestling

*Women's Gymnastics
    I: The Floor Exercise
    Event
*Women's Gymnastics
    II: The Vaulting,
    Balance Beam and
    Uneven Parallel Bars
    Events

BOOKS ON WATER SPORTS

*Canoeing
Powerboating
*Scuba Diving

Skin Diving and Snorkeling
Small Boat Sailing
Swimming and Diving

SPECIAL BOOKS

*Backpacking
Dog Training

Safe Driving
Training with Weights

*Expanded Format

# Sports Illustrated
# TUMBLING

**BY DON TONRY**
Illustrations by Don Tonry

**HARPER & ROW, PUBLISHERS, New York**
Cambridge, Philadelphia, San Francisco,
London, Mexico City, São Paulo, Sydney *1817*

FIRST EDITION

*Designer: C. Linda Dingler*

Library of Congress Cataloging in Publication Data

Tonry, Don.
  Sports illustrated tumbling.
  1. Tumbling. I. Sports illustrated (Time, inc.) II. Title. III. Title:
Tumbling.
GV545.T66 1982     796.4′7     82-47537
                   AACR2
ISBN 0-06-015022-X              83 84 85 10 9 8 7 6 5 4 3 2 1
ISBN 0-06-090984-6 (pbk)        83 84 85 10 9 8 7 6 5 4 3 2 1

# Contents

# Introduction

*Sports Illustrated Tumbling* has been written and illustrated for both the gymnast and the coach. It is meant to be used both as a day-to-day reference in the gymnasium and as an instructional text for serious private reading.

There is a tremendous amount of repetition inherent in any gymnastics text. The same or similar preparatory skills and movements often precede a newly introduced main skill. Also, the same biomechanical factors are often of equal importance in a variety of different skills. For these reasons I have chosen to place various comprehensive subjects at the beginning of the book. Other areas covered include a brief history of tumbling, spotting techniques, warmup, and post-training exercises. Although many of the views expressed in this book are commonly held by other experienced coaches, the majority are specifically my own.

Many gymnastics books contain instructional photos that often fail in sequence and timing; in this book, however, I have tried to capture the very essence of tumbling movements by basing my illustrations on accurate, carefully selected films of champions in action during competition. Hundreds of hours were spent studying these films before segments were chosen and reproduced on paper with the aid of an overhead projector. The results, I hope, are illustrations that will guide the coach and gymnast fluidly through skills of widely varying difficulty.

## TO THE COACH

You are coaching one of the most difficult sports in the world. You don't coach tumbling, or gymnastics, for that matter, by organizing drills, blowing a whistle or using a stopwatch. Rather, you coach it by physically manipulating bodies through the entire range of anatomical movement in all possible planes and axes. You must have analytical skill and a keen intuitive sense so you can solve both physical and emotional problems. Your attitude and expertise are the forces behind every training session and competition.

Aside from the technical-sequence illustrations, I hope you will find the sections on spotting, biomechanics, prerequisites, direction of movement, and general skill descriptions imaginative and informative. To get the most out of this book, I suggest that you periodically thumb back through earlier sections for reference to basic skills. As you'll see, certain starting positions and sequences are so similar that the *core skill,* from which they stem, should be reread to complete the descriptive package.

Spotting techniques are illustrated in an unusually detailed fashion, with text and illustration presented together.

Many skill descriptions are preceded by a brief paragraph that offers additional thoughts that relate to that skill. My intent is to suggest alternatives to the standard format of the description. You'll also notice that many of the advanced skills are only briefly described because the elements that comprise these skills have already been discussed, in some detail, on earlier pages.

Please note, too, that the point values assigned to various skills are strictly my own, and are meant simply to establish an approximate model for progression.

Virtually all the illustrations were drawn from film and present a high level of performance. In some cases, though, to provide an additional touch of realism, I have drawn some of the more basic skills from films of performers with limited tumbling experience. However, in no cases have I altered body forms or otherwise modified positions.

I hope this book will be a welcome addition to your library, will cultivate some new ideas, and perhaps reinforce some old ones.

# TO THE GYMNAST

If you're a beginner in tumbling, you may have difficulty understanding some of the material presented on biomechanics, twisting somersaults, elevation, and spotting. Although these areas will eventually be of great importance to you, they are intended for the more advanced student of the sport.

A beginning performer's chief goals should be developing an understanding of exercise, basic body position, progressions, prerequisites, and the functions of various specific body parts such as the head, eyes, arms, and legs. This book will lead you through many concepts and progressions that are meant to enhance your background for performing more advanced skills.

Chapter 7, "Exercise and Gymnastics," is intended to help you develop physical strength and flexibility for faster learning. Every beginning tumbler has his or her own physical limitations that can be eliminated or reduced through a program of progressive exercise training.

Chapter 8, "Basic Positions and Movements," will help you develop a clear understanding of the common body positions, jumps, and turns used during the performance of tumbling skills. If you take the time to learn all the material in this section, you will develop a strong base for other more difficult maneuvers.

Every skill has been given a "level" designation from 1 through 10, the purpose of which is to insure that you are learning a skill that relates to your ability level. Generally, you should learn all the skills in each level before moving on to higher level skills.

# 1

## Brief History

Tumbling activity dates back to prehistory. Although cave dwellers did not leave cave drawings demonstrating their interest in tumbling, we can safely assume that young people indulged in rolling, cartwheeling, and somersaulting, without instruction, as they do today. Later, more advanced societies left us pictorial accounts of "acrobats" performing inverted movements that can only be described as aerial maneuvers. These pictures are usually associated with festivals or exhibitions and generally depict a single nondescript skill.

Around 1810 in Germany, Friederich Ludwig Jahn (1778–1852) started a physical education movement that was based on natural outdoor activity. Jahn and his enthusiastic pupils invented games, various hanging and supporting apparatus, plus many new skills. Jahn's program eventually spread throughout Germany.

In the 1820s, three German refugees, Charles Follen, Charles Beck, and Francis Lieber, came to the eastern United States to escape political persecution—each was a protégé of Jahn. During the ensuing period, the Boston, Massachusetts area became the center for the prototype of the German *Turnvereine* (meaning "gymnastics association") movement, which later spread throughout

11

the country. In 1826, for example, Yale University, having heard of Harvard's gymnastics program, voted to build an outdoor gymnasium similar to Jahn's *Turnplatz* (or "gymnastics place") in Germany. Its conditioning apparatus consisted of bars, ropes, and poles. About thirty-five years later, Yale built a second gymnasium, containing a horizontal bar, vaulting horse, springboard, parallel bars, trapezes, flying rings, and landing mats. In January, 1873, a gymnastics instructor named Dudley Allen Sargent came to Yale and initiated one of the first collegiate exhibition gymnastics teams in the country. "The progress they made in tumbling and leaping amazed their instructor."*

From these early *Turnvereine*-oriented physical education programs sprang the sport that we know as gymnastics. During the same period, European gymnastics was undergoing a similar but more disciplined structural organization.

The first American Amateur Athletic Union national tumbling championships were held in 1886. Early tumbling routines were confined to handsprings, simple somersaults, and various acrobatic skills, and most gymnasts learned the sport without the benefit of coaching. Youngsters were able to surpass their predecessors so rapidly that invention and experimentation were the methods of improvement. Soft mats, trained coaches, and spotting devices, for all practical purposes, did not exist. Most skills were learned by trial and error. Today, an experienced coach with the proper equipment can teach youngsters skills in several weeks that formerly took months or years to master.

Over the years, American tumblers have led the world in the performance of advanced tumbling movements. In the 1932 Olympics, an American tumbler, Rowland Wolfe, won the gold medal. In the 1952 Olympics, Bob Stout was the first all-around gymnast to perform a full-twisting backward salto, or somersault, in the floor-exercise event. Four years later, in the 1956 Olympic Games in Melbourne, Australia, Abe Grossfeld showed the world full-twisting backward saltos in the floor-exercise, horizontal-bar, and still-ring events, and only an ankle injury prevented him from doing a double twisting salto on the floor. Two Americans, Sharon Richardson and Teresa Montefusco, demonstrated excellent full-twisting backward saltos in the 1960 Olympics, while European and Asian females were often having difficulty with simple layout saltos. Peter Kormann won a bronze medal at the 1976 Olympics with his introduction of the full-twisting double-backward salto. Peter was also the first American gymnast to win an Olympic medal since 1932. In the 1979 World

*George W. Pierson, "Apostles of Physical Culture," *Yale Alumni Magazine,* February 1973, pp. 12–17.

Championships, Kurt Thomas introduced the one-and-one-half twisting, one-and-one-half salto to international gymnastics. That year Kurt became the first American gold-medal winner in the floor-exercise event.

Two great American tumbling champions of particular note are Barbara Galleher Tonry and Judy Wills. Barbara won the national tumbling championships nine times, which makes her by far the winningest tumbler in American history. Judy Wills won only two national titles, but she will be remembered for her amazing feats of combination. Judy could perform over thirty "whip backs" in a series, five alternating double-twisting backs in a series, and many other mind-boggling combinations.

# Safety Techniques

## SPOTTING

*Spotting* is the term used to describe the act of giving physical assistance or being ready to give physical assistance to a gymnast during the course of performance. The functions of the spotter include: (1) instilling confidence in the performer, (2) providing safety, and (3) promoting correct body position during the performance of a skill.

### Hand Spotting

Two methods are commonly employed to spot a performer, and both are extremely functional when done correctly. The first method is called *hand spotting*—physically manipulating a performer through a movement. In this method the spotter grasps, pushes, or pulls a particular part of the body to encourage correct performance.

Some general considerations for hand spotting a tumbler include:

1. Establishing a *stable base of support* while spotting. This is usually accomplished by assuming a fairly wide stance and bending slightly at the knees and hips.

2. *Moving with the performer* so you are never caught in a position where you cannot apply maximum force if necessary.

3. *Moving close to the performer* so your leverage is maximized.

4. *Anticipating the forthcoming body positions* that the performer plans to assume.

5. *Anticipating the negative aspects* of the performance. You'll be faced at times with trying to avoid injury to yourself while still trying to be an effective spotter.

6. *Applying enough force* to administer the task. Although overspotting can be negative assistance, it is generally safer than underspotting.

7. Applying force in the *direction* (s) that enhances the motion of the skill. A performer will tend to take direction from the hand pressure you apply.

8. Applying force in relation to the natural *timing* of the skill. The performer will tend to follow your timing pattern.

9. Applying force on the *appropriate part of the body* to enhance the skill. If vertical support is necessary, support the hip area (center of gravity). If rotation is also necessary, guide and support another portion of the rotating body that is farther away from the center of gravity. When a performer is rotating on an external axis, such as the floor during a walkover, for instance, you will promote rotation by guiding any part of the body in the direction of rotation. However, the closer your guidance is to the axis of rotation, the less effective you will be. Thus, walkover-type skills are usually spotted from the hip and leg areas. Skills that rotate in free flight rotate around the center of gravity (internal axis). The spotter can best help the rotation by guiding a portion of the body that is away from the hip area.

## Belt Spotting

The second method of spotting is called *belt spotting.* Two methods of belt spotting are commonly used: the *hand-held belt* method and the *overhead traveling suspension belt* method. The hand-held belt technique is administered by two spotters holding opposite ropes that extend from the safety belt. As the performer runs down the mat, the spotters run along side and support the performer by holding the ropes. Although this method can be effective on simple skills, it requires two spotters and often interferes with the natural motion of the performer.

The overhead traveling suspension safety belt system is the safest and most reliable method of spotting. This method requires only one spotter and allows the performer a great deal of natural movement and excellent support. The

Spotting with the Overhead Safety Belt

traveling belt system acts as an extension of the spotter, thus keeping him or her clear of flailing arms and legs. Both performer and spotter are protected. Information on this system may be obtained from most gymnastics equipment manufacturers throughout the United States.

Use of the overhead traveling belt requires that the spotter move with the performer and take up slack in the ropes throughout the movement pattern. A very light spotter will generally find this system physically easier than hand spotting. The spotter works in reverse of the tumbler, pulling downward on the ropes as the performer moves upward. Landings are particularly easy to spot with this method because the spotter's leverage is greatly enhanced by the suspension system. Compared with hand spotting, it's also relatively easy to suspend a performer in midair in order to emphasize a particular body position.

## LANDING MATS AND LANDING PITS

Today's American tumblers have a distinct advantage over their predecessors and over most tumblers throughout the world. American industry and ingenuity have made possible various gymnastic learning devices that have permitted both a higher level of performance difficulty for the tumbler and greater safety. Multiple somersaults and twists, for example, may be practiced using a trampoline and safety belt; three or four different types of springboards are available for varying degrees of propulsion; landing mats come in four-, eight-, and twelve-inch thicknesses; spring floors are manufactured by many equipment companies; and safety pits are the vogue throughout the country. Some of these aids improve power at takeoff and others eliminate the hazards of landing.

The tumbler and coach "of old" had to contend only with hair-filled mats and a hand-held safety belt. Today, the myriad of equipment innovations both tempt us and allow us to perform difficult maneuvers. So, a word of caution when using modern equipment: go slowly. Carefully evaluate your level of ability before performing any difficult maneuver. Modern equipment can help you increase tumbling proficiency; it can also lull you into a false state of confidence. Use it wisely. Set realistic limits on what skills you'll try. The smart gymnast always underrates his or her ability just a little, to allow for any miscalculation.

The diagram shows several ways to use the twelve-inch landing mat in conjunction with a four-inch tumbling strip. The folded mat setup is generally used for forward tumbling skills to promote elevation during the salto (somer-

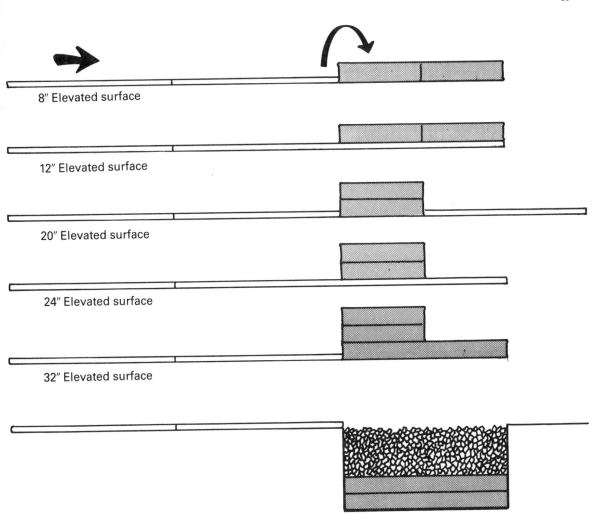

8″ Elevated surface

12″ Elevated surface

20″ Elevated surface

24″ Elevated surface

32″ Elevated surface

Landing Mats and Landing Pit

sault). Eventually, the performer should graduate to lower mat levels until ground-level performance is achieved.

The safety pit is an excellent training aid for twisting and double somersaults because it eliminates the hazards of landing in a position of underrotation. Still, landing-mat techniques require careful measurement of the distance the performer covers prior to takeoff; measurement is particularly important when using the safety pit because the risks, if the pit is missed, are greater. To insure consistent distance for preliminary movements (and to avoid injury), performers should always mark with tape their starting points on the running strip.

# 3

# Biomechanical Considerations

## A BRIEF LOOK AT BIOMECHANICS AND TUMBLING

Tumbling is a jumping activity. The tumbler jumps from hands to feet, from feet to feet, and from feet to hands. All these jumps are executed with rotation on an external axis (the mat) or an internal axis (the performer's center of gravity) in flight, and with linear motion (movement along the mat).

The power for tumbling movement comes from within the *muscle structure of the performer in combination with gravity.* The tumbler *forces himself or herself off balance,* allows the *force of gravity* to pull him or her toward the earth, and translates these forces into linear (straight-line) and rotary motion. When a tumbler jumps into a backward salto, or somersault, the height of the jump is determined by his or her speed, angle of takeoff, timing, and muscle force. Rotation is acquired simultaneously by the ground force acting in an equal and opposite direction to the leg push in unison with the arm thrust. A similar action would occur if you were to trip someone by kicking out the person's legs from the rear and simul-

21

taneously pushing the head backward. The result is backward rotation. Backward rotation also requires some backward lean; i.e., the ground reaction force generally passes slightly in front of the center of gravity as the tumbler executes the takeoff.

Once the tumbler leaves the ground, his or her flight path cannot be altered. The tumbler's center of gravity follows a parabolic curve. Its descent follows the same curved pathway as its ascent. The tumbler can, however, speed up rotation by contracting the length of his or her body. Thus, a tucked salto is easier to rotate than a layout salto where the performer's body remains straight. The most important point to remember in tumbling is that the power for elevation and rotation is established at takeoff. All saltos, at takeoff, start out as layouts, with more, or less, thrust for rotation. If the tumbler plans to execute a tuck from the layout, he or she simply emphasizes elevation at the expense of rotation knowing that contraction of the body into a tuck will cause rotation onto the feet.

Twisting rotation is most commonly initiated from the floor (surface of support) at takeoff. In this situation, the arms and torso thrust in the direction of the twist, causing the feet to push against the floor *in the opposite twisting direction*. Simultaneously, the floor pushes the performer into an opposite

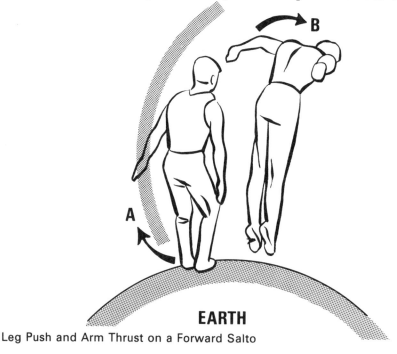

**EARTH**

Leg Push and Arm Thrust on a Forward Salto

twisting pattern that is *equal in magnitude* to the original thrust against the floor. This phenomenon is simply Newton's third law of motion: *For every force that is exerted by one body on another there is an equal and opposite force exerted by the second body on the first.*

**EARTH**

Leg Push and Arm Thrust on a Backward Salto

If the tumbler thrusts for twist with arms held wide apart, he or she has created the potential for multitwisting in relation to the strength of the initial thrust. Thus, the performer doing multitwists will have a slightly wider arm position as well as a slight increase in body turn at takeoff than the performer doing a single twist. Both factors insure the greater degree of twisting rotation the performer needs to achieve. When combining a twist with a salto, or somersault, the performer should always overemphasize the salto rotation because the length of the body makes rotation about the lateral salto axis much more difficult than twisting about the longitudinal twisting axis. Also, the initiation of the twist from the floor often causes a conflict of priorities (see p. 47, axes of rotation).

Other less common methods of initiating twists in tumbling are the *body-extension method* and the *asymmetrical-radius of rotation method*. These twisting methods are initiated by a change in body position in free flight, and do not require initiation from the floor at takeoff. In the former case, the body is forcefully extended from a tucked, piked, or pucked (open tucked) position *while somersaulting*. The portion of the body moving away from the direction of rotation (upper body in forward salto skills) is turned in the desired direction of the twist. The upper portion of the body is then stopped which causes a transfer of twisting momentum throughout the body as it straightens (straightening the body shortens the radius of twisting rotation). The lower portion of the body is then twisted in the same direction. As the body straightens, the rate of twist increases. This twisting technique may be observed on the piked backward salto with a full twist, which is illustrated on page 166 in this book.

The asymmetrical-radius of rotation twist results from shortening one side of the body (that is, lowering one arm) while somersaulting. The shortened side tends to rotate somewhat faster, which results in a small conversion of salto rotation to twisting rotation. If you are *rotating forward* and you lower your *right arm,* you will tend to twist *left.* If you are *rotating backward* and you lower your *right arm,* you will tend to twist *right.*

Consciously and unconsciously, the tumbler utilizes many twisting techniques. A twist off the floor is often aided by the asymmetrical-radius of rotation and the extension-twist techniques simultaneously.

Prior to landing, the tumbler must extend the limbs away from the axis of rotation in order to slow rotation. Thereupon, the foot placement on the mat must be at an angle that will cancel the rotation and linear motion to zero. If the tumbler wishes to keep moving in the same direction upon landing, the feet must be placed under the body at a lesser angle so continued motion is maintained. The tumbler must always judge the angle of foot placement in relation to linear and rotary speed. If the angle of foot placement is too great, it will retard movement in the same direction. If the angle is too little, the tumbler will probably be off balance in relation to the ensuing skill performance. All landings must also be accompanied by a flexion of the ankles, knees, and hips in order to absorb the shock of impact with the mat. The degree of flexion is determined by the amount of force that has to be absorbed and the strength of the performer. An analogous action occurs in baseball, when a catcher "gives a little" in order to reduce the magnitude of force of a moving ball. The catcher moves his glove backwards, increasing the distance of the stopping action, and thus softening the catch.

The tumbler is rarely in perfect control. Every movement or series of movements requires constant evaluation in order to compensate for some variable in performance. Most skills have a wide range of acceptable or functional performance. The tumbler must *react* and *adapt* to each phase, since it occurs somewhat differently in each trial. The good tumbler recognizes this and expects to make necessary adjustments with each performance.

## THE HEAD

In tumbling, the head functions mainly as the *carrier of the eyes and ears (equilibrium).* To a small degree, head weight does help salto rotation; however, its effect is minuscule when compared with the power and range of arm thrust. Biomechanically, head movement does not particularly help the tumbler in the performance of salto skills. Anatomically, the forward or backward posture of the head shifts the center of gravity. During twisting, the location of the head in the midline of the body (longitudinal axis) renders it, for all practical purposes, useless.

Generally, the placement of the head tells us the tumbler's *focus of orientation.* When the head is held in line with the body as the performer leaves the mat for a backward salto, we know that the focus is on the takeoff, and that the tumbler is most concerned with elevation. In the same way, if the tumbler's head is thrown backward at takeoff, we know the focus is on backward rotation and landing. Backward action of the head, in this case, also suggests insecurity and poor technical execution. Arm thrust should precede head thrust for improved elevation and rotation. The same example applies to twisting skills. If the head is turned into the twist at takeoff, we can guess that the performance will lack elevation and rotation because the focus is on finishing the twist rather than on jumping and somersaulting well.

## THE EYES

The eyes are our single most important guide for orientation. What a tumbler's eyes watch while she tumbles indicates her immediate area of concern. If they stop watching one phase of a skill and turn to the next phase, they are expressing concern for that next phase.

Every skill, then, should be considered in terms of optical orientation. Where and when should the tumbler look? Generally, the tumbler should *watch* (concentrate on) *the initiation of each skill* (jump or arm push), then look in the direction of the next phase. If the tumbler looks for the landing or twisting phase before the initiation of any skill is completed, the most important phase of the skill will be slighted.

## THE ARMS

The arms play an important role in establishing both salto and twisting rotation. The farther the arms are thrust away from the axis of rotation, in the direction of that rotation, the stronger that rotation will be. In tumbling, this action takes place in unison with the takeoff. With few exceptions, the tumbler initiates salto rotation and twist from the mat (surface of support).

A double-layout salto must have faster overhead arm thrust than a single-layout salto. A double-twisting backward salto must have faster and wider arm thrust than a single-twisting backward salto. Once the initial thrust has been established, the tumbler should shorten the *radius* of rotation by pulling the arms toward the *axis* of rotation. For the tumbler executing a layout salto, this means pulling the arms from overhead down to the hip area or out to the sides. Speeding up a twist requires that the tumbler pull the arms toward the vertical axis (generally the chest area) from a wide initial thrust. The arms must move quickly at takeoff in order to coordinate with the jump, then must be pulled in quickly to shorten the radius of rotation, which increases rotation speed.

## THE HIPS

The hip area supports the center of gravity, which is located approximately in the middle of the body at navel level. The elevation and direction of hip thrust at takeoff determine the route the tumbler will follow. If the hips are driven backward hard, the result will be a low salto or backward handspring. If they are projected high into the air from a near-balanced jump, the result will be a high salto. If they are turned at takeoff the body will twist.

The musculature in the hip area also plays a crucial role in tumbling. Every time we jump, we flex and extend our hips as well as our knees. The muscles that surround this multijoint area should be strong and flexible for maximum efficiency.

## THE LEGS

A tumbler's legs are the seat of his or her power. They must be strong and fast. Most of the legwork in tumbling is performed from a half bend (during handsprings) or slight bend (during saltos). Leg extension must coordinate with hip extension. The muscles in the thighs (quadriceps, hamstrings, adductors, etc.) span the knee as well as the hip area.

The natural weakness of the knee joint structure dictates that the tumbler be prudent, particularly when working on twisting skills. It doesn't take a great deal of sideward force to strain the knee joint. Trial-and-error twisting without a good spotter is not recommended.

The hip and leg muscles must also be strong for landing. Every landing should be accompanied by a hip and knee bend in order to absorb shock to the knee joint.

## CONSIDERATIONS FOR ELEVATION

The tumbler should recognize four basic biomechanical considerations for gaining elevation.

*Speed* in tumbling results from running forward in conjunction with a hurdle, or from moving backward from a tumbling series. The run, the hurdle, and the skills used to build up to a high jump must be accelerated in a straight line as the tumbler moves down the mat. Short, fast, backward handsprings do not cover much distance and therefore will not give you much linear speed to convert to elevation. The short backward handspring is analogous to running in place very fast. You certainly can't jump either high or far doing that type of run. How to get good speed doing any tumbling maneuver? The answer is to lean. As with the fast forward run, the hurdle, roundoff, and backward handspring should have optimum lean, but backward instead of forward. Just as in running, then, building speed in tumbling is a matter of increasing your lean (distance) and maintaining balance. If you lean too much, you will falter. If you lean too little, you will slow down.

The *angle* of contact with the mat is obtained through "blocking," which is the process of converting linear speed into elevation by driving your feet or arms into the mat at an angle contrary to the direction of motion. Blocking retards your action in one direction and sends it someplace else. The angle of the block determines where you will go. To demonstrate a block, try throwing a broom handle end first at the floor. Note that as the end hits the floor the broom handle bounds upward in relation to the speed of the throw and the angle of contact.

Our bodies are an improvement over the broom handle. We can add to this bounding action by using internal muscular force. The general rule is: If you've gained great linear speed during a maneuver, the angle of block should be greater.

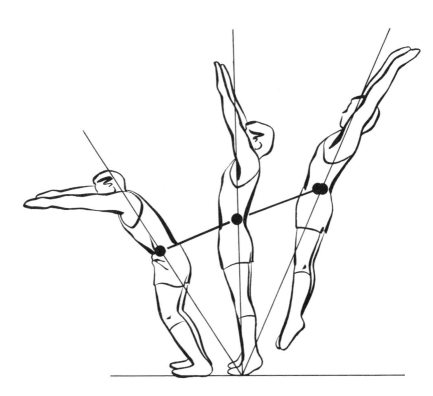

Blocking and Jumping for a Backward Salto

Poor Body Alignment for Jumping into a Backward Salto

*Timing* is one of the most critical factors in gaining correct elevation in tumbling. If our bodies were simple stiff broom handles we wouldn't have to worry about timing. Instead, we have an elastic structure that can either relax or produce a great amount of power in an instant. We are also composed of various body segments—arms, legs, head, torso—that must be coordinated and aligned in relation to our goals.

For example, upon landing from a backward handspring, the tumbler wishing to perform a high salto places his or her feet behind the hips (center of gravity). In other words, he or she blocks. At that point there is only a moment before the jump to elevate the body effectively. For that moment the tumbler is rotating backward on both feet, on the floor (external axis of rotation). As the center of gravity passes over the feet, the tumbler must jump, using correct body alignment and arm thrust. The tumbler generally leaves the mat with the center of gravity slightly behind the feet, and with arms driving for rotation (layout backward salto). *Many beginners fail to land from the backward handspring in a high enough position to jump within the limited effective time span.* The desire to jump at the correct time may be there, but the beginner must compensate for a low body position by arching the back in order to get the hips over the feet. The arch may be further exaggerated by the tumbler's desire to rotate backward, which generally requires the center of gravity to be somewhat behind the feet at takeoff. Arching also negates the overhead arm

30

Good Takeoff for Forward Salto from Forward Handspring

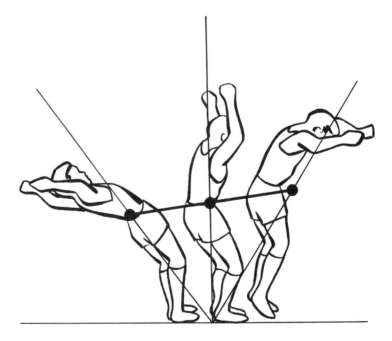

Poor Landing and Jump from Forward Handspring into Forward Salto

drive necessary for powerful rotation, because the arm drive must also accompany the jump. The beginner's low landing from a backward handspring makes leading with the arms almost impossible because the beginner is preoccupied with moving the center of gravity backward past the feet. In fact, good arm thrust from a very low position would probably destroy the salto altogether.

Thus, from the block off the handspring to the salto itself, timing is everything, and only good position guarantees good elevation in the limited time from one movement to the next.

*Muscular strength* enables a tumbler to jump high if all other factors—speed, angle, timing—are present. Heavy tumblers are at a disadvantage because they must apply more force to get the same job done. Therefore, they must be stronger than light tumblers.

A tumbler should mainly be concerned with leg strength for jumping, although the lower back is also an area of stress. Leg muscles must be able to respond quickly through a short range of motion with knees about half bent for handsprings, and even less for saltos.

Other muscle groups that deserve consideration are the arm extensors (triceps) and shoulders (deltoids). The tumbler's arms and shoulders, in effect, partially replace the legs on handsprings. They must also be able to handle the stresses of blocking and pushing away from the mat.

## POINTS TO REMEMBER

1. *The faster you move in a straight line down the mat, the greater your potential for elevation.* In other words, the tumbler's rate of stride and hurdle (hop and step), coupled with distance (length), will promote a jump for elevation. The length and rate of the movements used, prior to jumping, must be appropriate to the particular elevated skill. All skills performed prior to the elevated skill are "buildup" movements. During hurdles, round-offs, and handsprings, the body's center of gravity should be kept at an even level.
2. *The initiation of every skill is the skill's single most important phase.* The quality of the initial jump or thrust from the mat will determine the quality of the ensuing skill.
3. *Body curves and joint angles are effective springs for elevation and rotation.* The body's joint structure should be consciously flexed then extended, or vice versa, to promote elevation and rotation. The degrees of flexion and

extension should always be in relation to the performer's ability to use them.

4. *Optical orientation is the single most important orienting factor.* Every skill should be programmed for specific points of eye contact. Generally, try focusing on the support surface with as few optical shifts as possible.

5. *The farther the arms are from the axis of rotation, the greater the potential for rotation.* If arm thrust is coordinated with the jump, for example, driving the arms overhead will promote good salto rotation. Thereafter, stopping the arms and pulling them in toward the axis of rotation promotes further rotation. Twisting potential requires similar timing and procedure, with arms initially thrust sideward and held laterally at varying widths.

6. *When jumping for elevation, leave the mat with balanced body alignment.* During an effective jump, the body segments are aligned for total body projection. If a jump is initiated from an excessively arched or piked crouch, the ensuing jump will reflect the degree of misalignment.

7. *Head placement indicates a performer's primary concern.* The head is generally turned to accommodate the eyes, which are accommodating the brain. If a performer's head is thrown backward, prior to jumping for a backward salto, you can be sure he or she is more concerned with landing than with jumping.

8. *"Feeling" the performance of a skill is more important than mechanically assuming the correct body positions.* Multi-task skills require a total physical, emotional, and intellectual response. Physical effort is not enough.

9. *When twisting and somersaulting are incorporated in the same skill, the desire to twist tends to dominate the desire to somersault.* In order to combat this problem, the performer must learn to exaggerate salto rotation at takeoff.

10. *Drop the left arm for a right twist, when rotating forward. Drop the left arm for a left twist, when rotating backward.* Depending on the direction of the somersault, the shorter side of the body twists toward the longer side, because the shorter side rotates slightly faster.

11. *Every salto starts as a layout or untucked dive, with more or less thrust for rotation.* In other words, we must "follow through" with our jump into a salto before assuming a secondary tucked or piked position on saltos.

# Preparation for Projection

## SKIP-STEP HURDLE

In order for a tumbler's body to be in the correct starting position for forward handsprings, round-offs, and aerial saltos, he or she must hop on one foot and step to the other. This hopping and stepping action is called a *skipping hurdle*. The approach to the skipping hurdle may be a jump, a single step, a walk, or a run. There are two styles of skipping hurdles commonly used to initiate forward-moving, single-leg kicking skills.

### The Bent-Knee Style

The oldest and most common style of skipping hurdle is the *bent-knee style*. This hurdle is characterized by hopping on one leg while the other leg is brought forward and upward with the knee bent. Both arms are also brought forward in conjunction with the hop. The tumbler then first lands on the slightly bent hopping leg, and then steps forward onto a bending forward leg. This hurdle is usually performed when the main objective is to maintain forward running speed for a powerful series of movements. The hurdle is performed low and with a fair amount of forward lean in order to

33

Bent-knee Hurdle Style

closely simulate an extension of the run. Note, too, the body's center of gravity rises very little during the hopping phase of this maneuver compared to the straight-leg hurdle.

## The Straight-Leg Style

Often called a "European hurdle," the *straight-leg hurdle style* of skipping came into vogue in the early 60s. It was developed by European floor-exercise performers who felt the need to add expression to a simple skipping skill. Currently, both male and female performers use it as an aesthetic introduction to a single-leg kicking skill. It is characterized by a fairly high hop, with both legs joining in the air, prior to the landing on the hopping leg. The center of gravity rises and falls to a greater degree than during the bent-knee hurdle. This action retards forward speed, to some degree, which makes it less an extension of the forward run. It is used mainly with skills that do not require a great amount

of forward lean, such as high forward handsprings and aerial walkovers. In these instances, the straight-leg hurdle will often set the performer up for a more functional blocking action. The high hop tends to keep the performer's center of gravity slightly further behind the forward takeoff leg than the bent-knee hurdle style. Keep in mind that the hurdle is simply a preparatory movement for the skill that follows, and should be functional for a particular skill or skill series.

Learn the bent-knee style of hurdle first, because it is a clear extension of the common skipping action that most youngsters learn in various children's games, requires less motor coordination, and is functional for a greater variety of skills. For the performance of a cartwheel or roundoff, check to see which leg you wish to kick over your head first. If you wish to place your right hand down on the mat first (see illustration), you must first kick your left leg over your head. Your preliminary hurdle must then be executed with a hop on the left leg followed by a step forward on your right leg. Now you are in position

Straight-leg Hurdle Style

to kick your left leg over your head into a "right-hand-down-first" cartwheel or roundoff.

Once you've mastered the hurdle sequence from a *single step* (left), into a hop (on left) and step (on right), you're ready to add some additional preliminary walking steps before the hurdle. Practice swinging your arms forward and upward as you hop off your left leg.

As your hurdle improves, consider leaning forward as you hop, so you are falling slightly forward as you step forward with your right leg. A powerful step from a hurdle requires that your hopping leg *bend* as it lands on the mat, *after the hop.* This bent leg forcefully pushes against the mat as you step forward onto your right leg (also bent) for the final thrust.

The straight-leg hurdle follows the same sequence as the bent-leg hurdle, the only difference being the position of the body during the hopping phase. Study the illustrations and try copying the positions as carefully as possible.

## HURDLE TO A JUMP

The hurdle used in preparation for a jump should be an extension of your run. Remember, the actual distance the hurdle covers is related to the *speed of your*

*running approach* and the *angle of takeoff.* The purpose of the hurdle is simply to place both feet together, from a run, so you can jump in a desired direction with great force. Your hurdle should be low to the mat and therefore short. A high hurdle will obviously cover more distance than a low hurdle. The action of the hurdle itself is a negative force factor that must be used to create a necessary position for jumping high. Why negative? Because it retards the speed of the forward run to varying degrees, relative to how high it is executed. A low hurdle gives the performer more continuing speed from the run. Too low a hurdle, however, will not give the performer time to join both legs and rotate backward for a blocking action.

After your legs join for the jump, your feet should land in front of your hips, which, with your knees, should flex slightly. Foot placement (blocking angle) is determined by your forward speed. A slow run would require less blocking action for maximum efficiency.

The jumping action must be initiated immediately after the landing. This extension of the ankles, knees, and hips occurs so quickly that there is little, if any, pressure placed on the heels of the feet. The jump should be thought of as a spring from the balls of the feet.

The thrust of the arms should enhance the jump (see Arm Lift on Forward Salto Skills, page 39). To demonstrate the power of arm thrust, stand on a

Hurdle to a Jump

bathroom scale and raise your arms fast, stopping them abruptly. The corresponding shift in the scale reading is vivid proof of the elevation potential for arm lift when coordinated with jumping. Do not jump on the scale. Simply move your arms upward quickly.

On the other hand, if your arms are "out of sync" with your jump, they will not help your jump much at all. The elevating factor of arm lift depends upon its fast stopping. Biomechanically, when you stop your arm thrust, a transfer of momentum takes place whereby your arm-thrusting power is transferred through the rest of your body. In effect, the sudden stopping of your arms helps to pull the rest of you up.

When the tumbler first contacts the floor after the hurdle, his or her center of gravity is slightly behind the base of support. During the brief period from landing to jumping, the tumbler rotates on an external axis (the point where the feet are on the mat). As his or her center of gravity moves forward over the base of support, the tumbler must jump. At the moment of takeoff, the center of gravity is slightly in front of the base of support, to establish forward rotation.

Coaches, watch your tumblers' runs, hurdles, and jumps, paying special attention to speed, angle, and timing.

## ARM LIFT ON FORWARD SALTO SKILLS

There are three different types of arm lift commonly used to execute forward rotating skills originating from a two-foot takeoff. Each style emphasizes various factors such as elevation and rotation. The beginner is usually taught the *overhead throw* arm action because it provides a direct thrust into a pattern of forward rotation. When a beginner starts learning the forward salto, the biggest problem is proper rotation.

The second common method of arm lift is the *under lift*. Once performers master the knack of jumping into a pattern of forward rotation, they often change to the under lift in order to emphasize elevation. This is a more natural arm lifting action used on most simple vertical and long jumps.

The third and most recent (it was developed in the late 50s) arm lift is the *back lift*. This arm throw is literally the opposite of the under-lift technique. It affords excellent elevation and rotation because the arms thrust into the direction of rotation through a greater range of motion than with the other lifts. This technique was probably late in developing because it is unnatural and therefore tricky to learn. The idea of running forward and lifting backward tends to disorganize most beginners considerably.

## Overhead-Lift Arm Throw

(1–2) As you execute your hurdle, lift your arms overhead from your sides, keeping elbows slightly bent.

(3) Jump and simultaneously extend your elbows. Try to thrust your arms and shoulders as you jump.

This lift is generally used for handspring front salto combinations and diving handspring skills.

Overhead-lift Arm Throw

1    2    3

# Under-Lift Arm Throw

(1–3) As you execute your hurdle, raise your arms rearward from the sides. Then swing your arms forward, past your hips, just as you finish your two-foot landing.

(4) Your arms should be lifting forward and upward as the two-foot jump occurs. Try to feel the arms and shoulders lifting to aid the jump. The under-lift arm throw is the most common lift used for forward saltos and dive rolls.

Under-lift Arm Throw

1      2      3      4

## Back-Lift Arm Throw

(1–6) As you execute your hurdle, lift your arms overhead from your sides. Continue the arm swing forward and down so your arms swing rearward past your hips as the landing occurs.

(7–8) Continue the arm lift to approximately the shoulder level. By the time you leave the mat with your toes, your arms are about shoulder high in the rear.

This lift is commonly used for dive rolls and forward saltos. It is considered the most efficient lift for forward saltos from a run.

Back-lift Arm Throw

1

2

3

4

5

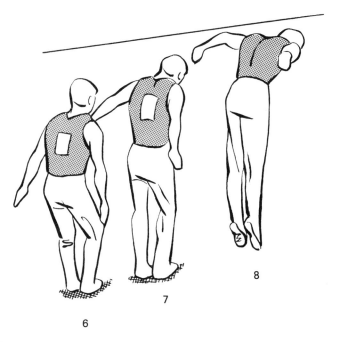

6

7

8

# 5

# Direction of Movements

## CRITERIA FOR TWISTS AND SALTOS

Before discussing the direction of movement in gymnastics, let's look at the term *center of gravity*. The center of gravity is the center of mass of any object. Though it varies with each individual because of physical structural differences, the center of mass in the human body is located roughly midway between the backbone and the navel (Fig. 1). If you are top-heavy, your center of gravity is slightly higher than that of a person who is bottom-heavy. If you raise your arms overhead, your center of gravity moves slightly higher (Fig. 2). If you change your body position (e.g., when piking), your center of gravity moves slightly forward, out of your body, and toward your knees (Fig. 3).

When your body is in free flight it twists or somersaults around an *internal axis* that passes through your center of gravity. For practical reasons, three axes of rotation are generally considered. The *lateral axis* runs from side to side (forward and backward saltos) (Fig. 4). The *anterior-posterior axis* runs from front to back

47

1

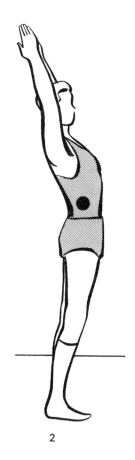

2

3

The Lateral Axis

The Anterior–Posterior Axis

The Longitudinal Axis

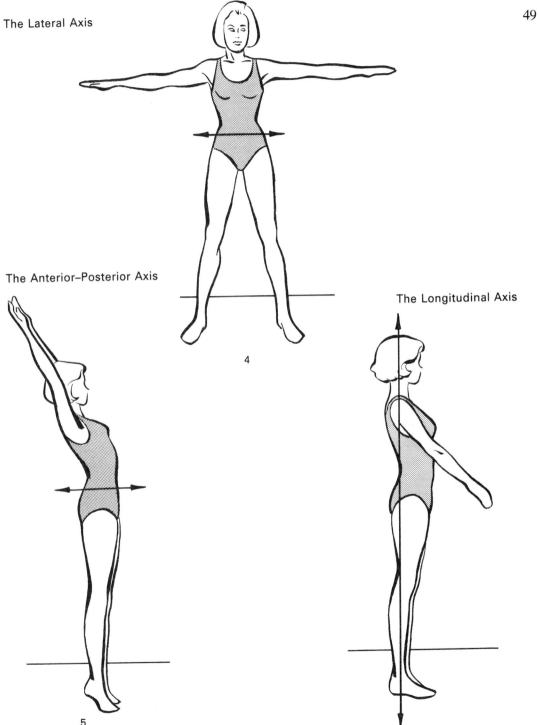

4

5

6

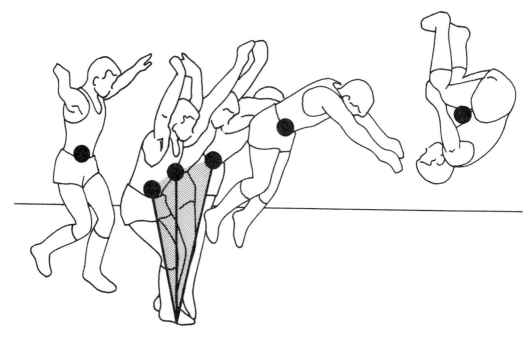

The Center of Gravity on a Jump into a
Forward Salto

(side saltos) (Fig. 5), and the *longitudinal axis* runs from head to foot (twisting skills) (Fig. 6).

When the gymnast rotates while being supported by the floor or a bar, rotation occurs on an *external axis*—the floor or bar. For instance, upon landing on the mat prior to a jump into a forward salto, you rotate forward on an external axis (the mat) for a moment prior to the jump. As you leave the mat and move into free flight, you rotate on an internal axis that passes through your center of gravity (see illustration). So the act of tumbling becomes a process of ever-shifting internal and external axial rotations.

Direction of movement has confused coaches and gymnasts for many years. Most authors choose either to ignore or circumvent the subject. In the course of perusal through a vast catalogue of gymnastics material, I came upon a book that was written almost one hundred years ago. I offer the following from *Gymnastics* by A. F. Jenkins,* an Englishman, who in 1887, 1888, and

*Frederick A. Stokes Company: New York, 1890.

1889 won the German Gymnastics Society's Challenge Cup. The date of publication was 1890.

The meaning of the expressions "turn to the right" and "turn to the left" must be clearly understood. Imagine that you are standing on the face of a clock at the centre, and that you turn with the hands; you turn to the right; if you turn in the opposite direction, you turn to the left. Now suppose you are not upright, but in some other position; imagine that your legs are in a straight line with the body, with the feet against the face of a clock; then, if you turn with the hands, you turn to the right; if in the opposite direction, you turn to the left. For example, if you are lying down on your back and roll over on to your right side, you turn to the right. Again, if you are lying down on your face and roll over on to your right side, you turn to the left.

The word "turn" in gymnastics language, used with reference to the body, is confined in meaning to a rotation about an axis parallel to the backbone. You often, of course, in doing exercises perform a rotation about axes in other directions; for example, in movements in the course of which you turn head over heels, such as circles on the horizontal bar, you perform a rotation about an axis parallel to the straight line joining the points of the shoulders; but such a rotation is not called a turn.

A rotation about the last mentioned axis is denoted by the words "swing," "circle," "roll," or "somersault," and the rotations in two directions are distinguished by the use of the words "forwards" and "backwards," or "front" and "back." In all forward or front circles, rolls, or somersaults, the rotation is with the hands of a clock placed on your left with the face toward you; in backward circles, rolls, or somersaults, the rotation is against the hands of a clock so placed. In forward swings, however, the rotation is in the same direction as in backward circles, rolls or somersaults; and in backward swings the rotation is in the same direction as in forward circles, rolls, or somersaults.

It may be advisable to point out that it is at first by no means easy to see which way you should turn to do a right turn when in a vertical position with the legs above the head, for example, in a handstand. If you are in a handstand on the parallel bars, and turn to a handstand on the left bar, placing the right hand in front of the left, so that the thumbs of the two hands are next to each other, you have done a quarter *right* turn. This seems surprising at first, but a little thought will convince you that it is so.

If you have difficulty understanding the last few paragraphs, I should advise you to cut a rough figure of a man out of a piece of paper, and mark his face and back, and his right and left arms and legs, then draw an arrow across his chest with the point towards his right shoulder, and then remember if he is turning so that the arrow is moving in the direction in which it is pointing, he is turning to the right, and you will easily convince yourself by experiment that the statements in these paragraphs are accurate.

I offer Mr. Jenkins's explanation of direction of movement as a pleasant surprise. His explanation of *twisting direction* is particularly appropriate in view of the confusion that often exists concerning twisting direction in an inverted position. Sixty-seven years (1957) after Jenkins's book was published, Abe Grossfeld (1956 and 1960 Olympic teams) made the same observation while performing a barani on the trampoline. Abe perceived that a barani (which is analogous to a left-hand-down-first roundoff) is really a half twist to the right. Therefore, he decided that all roundoff type actions (such as inverted pirouettes) that move in a similar pattern are right twists. Initially, this observation was rejected by some of the best coaches in the business. Finally, after many years of presenting this twisting dilemma to coaches and gymnasts at clinics throughout the country, it has become an accepted standard when discussing twisting.

## WHICH DIRECTION SHOULD I LEARN TO TWIST?

This question has plagued coaches and performers since the early days of tumbling. The answer isn't easy because it relates to factors that often seem inconsistent with natural motion. The problem may be stated in the following manner: The direction in which the performer would *like* to twist may be in conflict with the direction the performer *must* twist in in order to step from one skill directly into the next.

The performer should twist all forward and backward salto (i.e. somersaulting) skills in a direction consistent with a *stepout* into a forward handspring or a roundoff. For this reason, it is often beneficial for the coach to test a beginning tumbler's directional twisting preference before teaching a cartwheel, a roundoff, or a forward handspring. This can be done with a fair amount of accuracy by having the performer execute a full twist with a vertical jump, and a full twist from a prone and supine position. Once the favored direction, left or right, has been established, the pushing leg on that same side should be used on cartwheels, roundoffs, and forward handsprings. Thus, for example, the left pushing leg on a roundoff translates into a left twisting direction on somersaults.

Admittedly, some performers will find that they would rather push into a handspring movement with the leg opposite the desired twisting direction. However, "natural" twisting direction assumes more priority as a tumbler becomes more advanced. Besides, roundoffs and handsprings are only introductory skills that prepare the tumbler for more difficult advanced tumbling skills.

Generally, the performer who feels most comfortable performing a "left-hand-down-first" cartwheel or roundoff will tend to feel comfortable executing

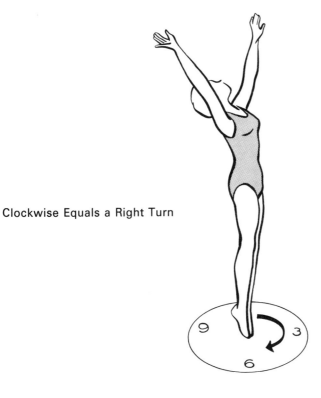

Clockwise Equals a Right Turn

The Face of a Clock Faces the Performer on Side Saltos

Clockwise Equals a Forward Salto

twisting skills to the left, and vice versa. Occasionally this rule does not hold true because of a performer's other experiences or abilities. Some performers will say that they have a particular favored twisting direction because they "think" that is the way they should twist. Often, their opinion is based on some totally unrelated factor (such as being right-handed) that does not necessarily explain their innate desire to twist one way or the other. Performing gymnastics skills requires a total mind-body commitment unique to each individual. Situations arise when rules and principles must be changed to suit special individual needs.

Generally, do not learn forward salto twisting skills as extensions of a barani (a forward salto with an early half twist). Most performers execute the barani in the same twisting direction as their roundoff. The roundoff twist direction should be opposite the direction used for salto twists. Performing the roundoff in the opposite twisting direction is necessary for stepping into a handspring movement from a forward or backward twisting salto. *Forward twisting skills that finish with a stepout must be twisted in the same direction as backward twisting skills, in order to continue stepping into a roundoff or forward handspring.*

# The Importance of Prerequisites

Below, the reader will find descriptions of a series of prerequisite skills. The student should take the time to learn these skills before moving on to the principal illustrated skill. The theory of prerequisites tells us that a broad range of easier related skills should be mastered before going on to a specific, more difficult skill. In this instance, our goal will be learning a tucked forward salto, or somersault, to a stand.

## LEARNING THE FORWARD SALTO

The basic technique requirements include (1) leaping from one foot to two feet, i.e. doing a hurdle, (2) jumping while moving forward, (3) establishing forward rotation from a jump, (4) tucking, (5) orientating while tumbling forward, and (6) landing with control. Any of these factors not developed to a high level will weaken the forward salto pattern and inhibit excellent performance. Here are a series of prerequisite skills commonly used to build up to performing an excellent forward salto.

55

**STEP ONE**

### Jump to a Forward Roll on High Mats (24″ high)

Standing on a vaulting board with your arms held overhead and elbows bent, jump to a forward roll. Your knees should straighten as you jump and your hands should not touch the mat until your feet have left the vaulting board.

### Multiple Jumps to a Forward Roll

Execute three fast jumps, in place, to a forward roll. The multiple-jump technique should teach you how to rebound off a hard surface into a dive roll.

### Step and Leap into a Jump to a Forward Roll

Take one or a short series of steps, and leap from one foot into a jump off both feet and into a dive roll. Stepping and leaping into a two-footed jump is the hurdle technique used for a running forward salto.

Jump to a Forward Roll on High Mats

### Forward Salto to a Sitting Tucked Position

Stand on the vaulting board with your arms overhead and elbows bent. Simultaneously, jump and extend your elbows. As you jump from the board, your arms, head, and upper back round forward as if you were throwing a basketball from behind your head. Finish in a sitting tucked position with your hands holding your knees. Note that you must keep your knees apart for the landing in the sitting tucked position. If you don't keep your knees apart, your face may hit your knees as you land—ouch! This drill will teach you how to jump and rotate at the same time.

### Multiple Jumps to a Forward Salto to a Sitting Tucked Position

Stand on the vaulting board with your arms overhead and elbows bent. Jump three times, then do a forward salto and land, sitting, with knees apart. This drill helps you develop the feeling of rebounding directly into a pattern of forward rotation.

Forward Salto to Seat on High Mats

## Step and Leap into a Jump to a Forward Salto to a Sitting Tucked Position

Take one or a short series of steps to a leap from one foot into a jump off both feet and into a forward salto. Land in a sitting tucked position with knees held apart. This drill incorporates the hurdle with the jump into forward rotation.

## Step and Leap into a Jump to a Forward Salto

Take a short series of steps into a hurdle. Jump into a forward salto and attempt to land on your feet. You should release your knees just before landing. If you are experiencing difficulty rotating to your feet, examine the weakest phase and relearn.

## Forward Salto on Lower Mat Level (12″ high)

Repeat the last step, but this time with mats at a lower level. You should be finishing in a fairly erect standing position at this stage of your training.

# STEP THREE

## Repeat Salto Stages without the Use of the Vaulting Board

Start with multiple jumps in place and go into a forward salto. Work your way up to a short run and hurdle into a forward salto. If you have learned each technique well, the forward salto should be yours.

# LEARNING THE HANDSTAND

Every tumbler should learn a handstand for general control in the inverted position. The floor-exercise performer must learn a handstand because of the variety of skills that utilize that position. This section will also demonstrate the concept of prerequisite skill development. As stated earlier, the theory of prerequisites tells us that a broad base of easier skills should be mastered before going on to other more difficult *movement-related skills.* In this instance we are dealing with the goal of learning a handstand. The problem is maintaining *balance* in an inverted position. Here are a series of balance skills commonly used as prerequisites for learning a handstand.

## Knee-Elbow Headstand

(1) Squat with your knees apart. On the mat, place your hands about shoulders' width apart) between your knees and with your fingers spread.
(2) Rest the inner part of your knees on your elbows or upper arms. Bend your elbows further and carefully place the top part of the front of your head on the mat about eight inches in front of your hands. Hold for five seconds and return to the starting position.

Knee-elbow Headstand

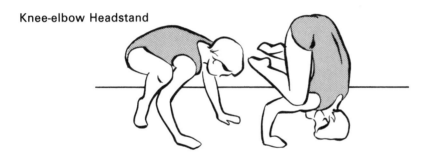

## Knee-Elbow Handstand

This skill is performed in the same manner as the knee-elbow headstand but the head is *not* placed on the mat. Instead, you must balance on your arms while watching the mat area in front of your hands. Hold for five seconds and return to the starting position.

Knee-elbow Handstand

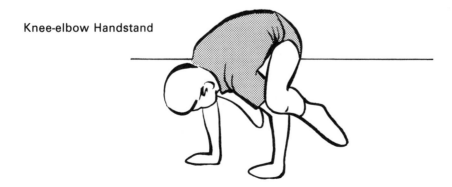

# Headstand

(1) Squat with your hands on the mat about shoulders' width apart. Place your head (between the crown and hairline) on the mat about eight inches in front of hands. Your hands and head now form a triangular base of support for balance. Extend one leg to the rear.

(2) Carefully push with your bent leg and raise your extended leg over your head. Your body weight should shift to your arms and head as the toe of the pushing leg leaves the mat.

(3) Raise the pushing leg to the high leg. You will feel most of your weight shift from your arms to the middle of your triangular base as your legs join. Once you are stable, most of your weight should be over your head. It is important to keep your neck and trunk straight for correct body alignment.

Headstand

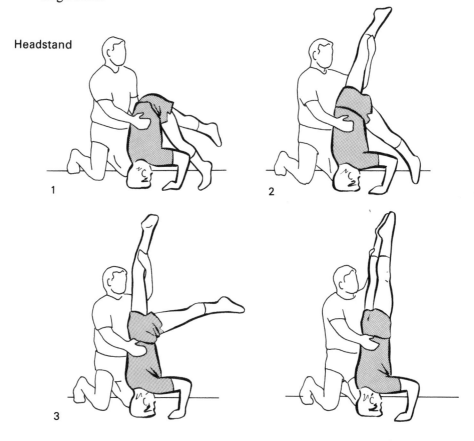

1

2

3

# Forearm Stand

Place your forearms on the mat about shoulders' width apart. With one leg bent and the other extended to the rear, kick your extended leg over your head. You should have a spotter catch your leg and stabilize your position. Bring your other leg up to your high leg. Keep your upper arms vertical at all times. If your shoulders sag forward, you will lose your balance and fall forward. Balance by subtly shifting your shoulders forward and backward as the need arises.

Forearm Stand

# Handstand

The ability to hold a handstand requires a couple of months' consistent practice. Providing you've mastered the prerequisites, the number of handstands that you try will determine how quickly you master this skill. Generally, the gymnast who seriously tries to hold fifteen handstands every day will learn a handstand faster than the gymnast who attempts only five a day.

Practice your handstand against a wall until you can balance on your hands for a few seconds at a time. Learn to move your feet off the wall by pressing with your fingertips against the floor.

Before proceeding to non-wall training, be sure that you can safely *cartwheel* out of your handstand when an *over-balance* occurs. Learn this *recovery movement* by having a spotter support and turn your hips into a cartwheel as you fall over.

Always practice your handstand from a stationary single-leg squat position until your inverted balance becomes fairly consistent. The illustration shows the handstand being practiced from a stand in order to develop the relationship between a kick to a handstand and a kick to a forward handspring.

Handstand

# 7

# Exercise and Gymnastics

The sport of gymnastics—tumbling in particular —utilizes every muscle in the human body in a more aggressive fashion than almost any other activity. In general, the concept of physical fitness embodies a series of functions, including strength, balance, flexibility, agility, endurance, coordination and kinesthetic awareness. The concept of *total fitness* includes the additions of physiological fitness and psychological fitness. A good athlete must be totally fit in order to excel in a particular sport. Physical, physiological, and psychological fitness all interweave in varying degrees with each athlete and with each sport. Long-distance runners, for instance, must have a high level of physiological fitness in order for the body chemistry to accommodate prolonged respiratory stress. Psychologically, runners must be able to maintain the desire to run under conditions of stress, and even physical pain.

Every sport requires varying levels of fitness. Assuming basic health, a gymnast is primarily concerned with physical and psychological fitness because these are the areas of greatest stress. Physically, a good tumbler must have fair strength, excellent balance, fair flexibility, excellent agility, fair muscular endurance, excellent co-

63

ordination, and excellent kinesthetic awareness. Psychologically, a good tumbler must be able to cope with the pressure of fear by linking up the physical (ability) with the emotional (confidence).

This chapter is concerned with only a small segment of the overall picture of *physical fitness*— strength, flexibility, and muscular endurance. The other factors—agility, balance, coordination, and kinesthetic awareness—are somewhat harder to improve because they are closely akin to innate physical ability.

The exercises I present may be considered for the all-around gymnast as well as the tumbler or floor-exercise specialist. The body positions and number of repetitions that I suggest will, of course, vary according to your physical makeup and tolerance for exercise. But remember, some degree of stress is essential in order to condition the body for greater ranges of motion and muscular overload. The key danger sign to watch for while exercising is pain. If it hurts, ease off or stop. Remember, you're trying to condition yourself for improvement, not rehabilitation.

*Specificity* is also important in exercise. Concentrate on those exercises that are most closely related to the problems that you are experiencing as a tumbler. If, for example, your shoulders sag while doing handsprings, do more shoulder extension exercises that move through the same range of motion as the handspring. With your coach, evaluate your weaknesses and together develop a program of exercise tailored to your tumbling needs. The rule of specificity also tells us that because tumbling is a fast-moving activity performed over a short period of time, you should perform strength exercises quickly, in order to build power for fast movement. As you change from one exercise to another, choose strength exercises that stress different muscle groups so you won't have to rest between sets. Also, use the overload principle in your strength training. Do high numbers of repetitions to make your muscles move faster and improve their endurance, and do that extra repetition to build your muscles' strength.

For the greatest improvement, flexibility training must also be specific. The stretching exercises I present go far beyond a tumbler's needs. They are designed more for the floor-exercise specialist or all-around gymnast who must incorporate a wide range of motion into various joint areas. If you are strictly a tumbler, you may wish to disregard the extreme straddle stretching and extreme shoulder-stretching exercises. Move slowly when practicing your flexibility exercises or you may pull a muscle. The current recommended procedure for stretching is to hold a slightly uncomfortable stretching position for five to twenty seconds. The stretch is then repeated several times with brief periods of rest in between. You will find yourself able to move into a lower stretched position with each repetition. Never have someone force you out of your range of motion unless it is slow and under your complete control. As a gymnast you must learn the difference between pain and simple discomfort. Pain hurts; discomfort causes only some soreness.

## WARMUP EXERCISES

Stretch the Calf Muscles and Jog at the Beginning of Your Warmup

### Calf Stretch

Place both hands against a wall and step backward with one foot until you can barely place weight on your heel. Gently press your heel to the floor. Hold this position for ten seconds. Change feet and execute on the other foot. Repeat about five times. You may also execute the calf stretch from a pushup position as illustrated. This exercise will increase the range of motion in your ankle and condition the calf muscle for the stress of jogging.

### Jogging

Jog forward and backward until you breathe heavily or even break out in a light sweat. This should not take more than five minutes. Some experts feel that jogging backward helps to warm up and strengthen the anterior tibialis muscles of the lower leg, and could prevent shin splints. The jogging warmup helps flush blood through your system which, accompanied by other chemical reactions, produces a warming effect. Cold muscles are more likely to tear under stress. When an inactive muscle is stimulated repeatedly, the early contractions are often weak and irregular. Relaxation of the muscle is also often retarded. Warm muscles contract and relax faster. The force and regularity of contraction is also improved.

## Side Stretching

Side Stretching

Stand with legs apart and gently stretch upward and side-downward with a gentle bouncing motion as illustrated. Execute about ten times on each side.

## Hamstring Stretching

"V" Sit Stretch

### "V" Sit Stretch

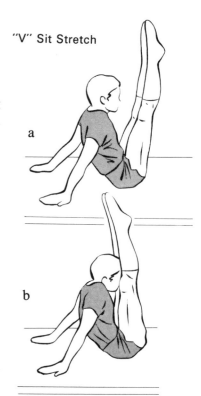

Sit on mat with hands behind hips as illustrated. Raise legs upward toward face without bending them. Flex feet at the ankle (hook toes), if you wish, to increase the stretching action in the hamstring and calf area. If you are very flexible in this position (see illustration b) you will be able to put your knees against your face. This is a good beginners' stretching exercise because the thigh muscles (quadriceps) regulate the tension on the hamstrings, thus making it almost impossible to pull a muscle. Practice holding your legs as close to your face as possible three times for five seconds each time.

a

b

### Squat Stretch

Put your legs in a straddle position and squat with hands on the mat. Straighten one leg by increasing the bend in the other knee. Gently bounce in the direction of the straight leg five times and repeat on the other side. This is a slightly more aggressive stretching exercise than the "V" sit stretch because your legs are bearing the weight of your body. Use your arms to regulate the pressure on the extended leg.

Squat Stretch

## Piked Stretch

Sit on the floor, or stand with feet together and legs straight. Bend forward at the waist and try to put your face on your legs. You may grasp your legs in either position and gently assist the stretch. Hold in a fairly uncomfortable position for ten seconds. Relax and repeat four times.

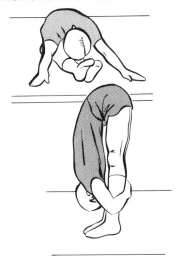

## Split Stretch

Slowly slide to the floor with one leg in front of the other. Place your hands on the sides of your front leg as illustrated. Gently lower your body to a fairly uncomfortable position and hold for ten seconds. Repeat with other leg forward. Do this five times on each side. A complete split requires conscientious training over a period of six months or more. Women tend to be naturally more flexible than men in this position because of pelvic structural differences. It is fairly easy to pull a muscle in this position because most of your weight is pressing you downward. Go slowly.

Split Stretch

## Split and Stretch

Once you have mastered the split, you may want to stretch even further. You can create greater stretch by resting your face against your front leg. If you hook your front toes, you will feel even greater stretch. Practice holding this position for ten seconds at a time on both sides. Three repetitions on each side should improve hip and leg flexibility after several weeks.

Split and Stretch

## Adductor Stretching

The adductor (inner-thigh) muscles are located so close to the hamstring (rear-of-thigh) muscles that they are often stretched together in various exercises. If your hamstring muscles are tight, you will probably find some of the adductor exercises difficult.

### Knee Press

Knee Press

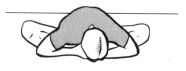

Sit on the mat and bend both knees as much as possible. Gently press your knees out to the side and place the soles of your feet together. Grasp your feet with both hands and pull feet closer to your hips. Bending gently, try to put your face on your feet while pressing knees downward toward the mat. Hold in a fairly uncomfortable position for ten seconds. Relax and repeat four times. This is a good exercise for beginners because it is easy to control the downward pressure.

### Straddle Front Rest

Straddled Front Rest

Sit and spread your legs as far apart as possible. Gently bend forward and place your stomach and chest on the floor. This is a combination adductor-hamstring exercise. As you learn to hold your legs directly out to both sides it becomes almost pure adductor stretch. Hold the bent position for ten seconds. Relax and repeat four times.

### Side Split

Side Split

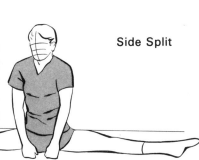

Stand with legs apart. Bend forward and place hands on the floor for support. Slowly slide legs further apart until you are in your lowest split position. This is a combination adductor-hamstring exercise. Sometimes the depth of the socket (fossa) in the hip will prevent the thigh bone (femur) from rotating outward enough to allow you to assume a complete sitting position. Carefully hold your lowest position for ten seconds. Relax and repeat four times.

## Shoulder Stretching

### Bend and Stretch

With both hands, grasp a bar around chest level and with a wider-than-shoulder-width grip. Bend forward, with legs straight, and gently press shoulders downward. Hold in a slightly uncomfortable position for ten seconds. Relax and repeat four times. This is a good exercise for beginners because the stretch is fairly passive.

Bend and Stretch the Shoulders

### Shoulder Rotation

With both hands, reach backward and grasp a bar palms down, around shoulder level ( A ). If your shoulders are not very flexible, your hands should be wide apart. Now, bend your knees and push away from the bar through your shoulders ( B ). Gently rotate your shoulders forward as you move below the bar ( C ). Repeat this movement four times. Be very careful. Learn to master the technique of rotating your shoulders without undue stress.

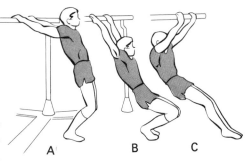

Shoulder Rotation Stretch

### Horizontal Stretch

Assume a rear support position. Have a partner grasp your legs and gently pull you forward to a fairly uncomfortable position. Hold for five se-

Horizontal Shoulder Stretch

conds. Return to the starting position and repeat four times.

## Hip and Shoulder Stretching

Bridge Position

### Bridge

Bridge Position

Rest on back with knees bent and apart. Place hands under shoulders with fingers facing toward feet. Gently push with arms and legs until hips raise as high as you can hold them. (Most people find this position very difficult; some are never able to straighten their arms and legs as illustrated.) Hold your highest position for five seconds. Relax and repeat four times. Beginners should slowly work up to five repetitions over a period of several weeks.

### Handstand Snapdown

This warmup exercise is for the performer soon to learn a backward handspring. Learn a fairly stable handstand position before attempting this drill.

Kick to a near handstand position with your back arched. Bend your knees and allow your shoulders to sag slightly. Quickly straighten your legs and pike downward, extending shoulders vigorously. Land with your feet under your hips and your arms held forward in front of you. Your soles should land about two feet from your original hand position on the mat. Practice five handstand snapdowns before every workout.

Handstand Snapdown

# POST-TRAINING EXERCISES

Post-training exercises are meant to be strenuous. They are a valuable addition to your gymnastics training, and are designed to strengthen general and specific muscle groups. The gymnast must choose the exercises that best suit his or her needs. The tumbler is mainly concerned with shoulder strength (deltoids), arm extensor strength (triceps), stomach strength (abdominal area), upper leg strength (quadriceps) and lower leg strength (gastrocnemius). Post-training exercises should be performed three times a week, throughout the year, if possible. Because we are dealing with maximum stress, the body will need a day of recuperation between exercise sessions. You can expect to be a bit sore on the days following your post-exercise training sessions. Enjoy your soreness because it means your strength is improving, and improved strength means improved gymnastics.

Pullups

## Pullups (Latissmus dorsi, Biceps)

Although the tumbler does not require the pulling strength of the all-around gymnast, a balanced exercise training routine should include this exercise on a regular basis.

Hang on a bar with palms forward. Stretch as much as possible from the shoulders and hips. Pull upward with a smooth motion until your chin is above the bar. Lower and repeat until you cannot perform any more. Beginners should have assistance.

## "V" Ups (Abdominal Area)

This exercise is an alternate to hanging toe touches and is meant for the less experienced tumbler. The ability to pike quickly and deeply is important in almost all gymnastics events. Do this exercise as quickly as possible and with good form.

"V" Ups

Rest on back with arms behind head. Raise upper and lower body simultaneously to toe-touch position. Do as many as you can, as fast as you can.

Hanging Toe Touch

## Hanging Toe Touch (Abdominal Area)

This is a heavy-duty abdominal exercise that beginners will find difficult.

Hang on a bar with palms forward. Stretch in the shoulders and hips. Raise legs smoothly to the bar until ankles touch. Lower and repeat until you cannot do any more.

Hanging Tuckups

## Hanging Tuckups (Latissmus dorsi, Abdominal Area)

Hang on a bar with palms forward. Stretch from the shoulders and hips. Bend knees and hips with a slow curling motion until your ankles touch the bar. Repeat as many times as possible. Beginners may have to swing up from an arched hang.

## Dips (Triceps, Latissmus dorsi, Pectorals)

Dips

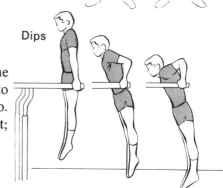

Assume a straight-arm support position on the parallel bars. Bend elbows and lower shoulders to the lowest position. Repeat as many as you can do. Women may find this exercise extremely difficult; in that case, substitute pushups for dips.

## Pushups (Pectorals, Deltoids, Triceps)

This exercise is an alternative to dips for less experienced performers.

Assume a front support position as illustrated. Hold body very straight. Bend your elbows until your chest gently presses against the floor. Repeat as many times as possible.

## Handstand Dips (Deltoids, Triceps)

Handstand Dips

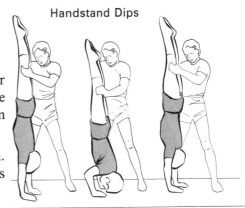

This exercise should be performed with a partner or with your feet resting against the wall. The advanced male performer may choose to perform without assistance on the low parallel bars.

Assume a straight body handstand position. Bend elbows and lower head to the mat. Repeat as many times as possible.

## Vertical Jumps (Quadriceps)

Vertical Jumps

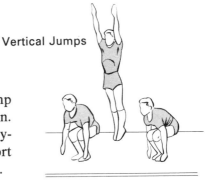

Squat with hands on the floor for support. Jump as high as possible and return to starting position. Never allow your knees to bend more than forty-five degrees and always use your hands for support as you land. Repeat as many times as possible.

## Static Arch (Lower Back, Hip Extensors)

Static Arch

This is a relatively mild static exercise that strengthens the lower back and teaches a tight arched position.

Lie on your back with arms held backward overhead. Push against the floor with your heels, tuck your hips under, and squeeze your seat muscles together. Hold your hips as high as possible for ten seconds without relaxing your tight hip position. Repeat four times.

## Static Hollow on Back (Hip Flexors)

Static Hollow on Back

This is a mild hip flexor exercise that teaches a tight hip, hollowed body position.

Rest on your back with arms held obliquely overhead. Tuck your hips under so your lower back is flat on the floor. Squeeze your seat muscles together tightly and curl your upper body and legs upward so you are only resting on your lower back. Hold this position for ten seconds and repeat four times.

## Static Hollow on Front (Hip Flexors)

Static Hollow on Front

This is a fairly strenuous hip flexor exercise that teaches a tight hip, hollowed body position.

Lie facedown with arms held obliquely out to the side. Flatten lower back by pulling stomach in and squeezing seat muscles together. Push against floor with forearms and toes. Raise trunk about four inches off floor and hold for ten seconds. Repeat four times.

# Straight Body Raise (Hip Alignment Drill)

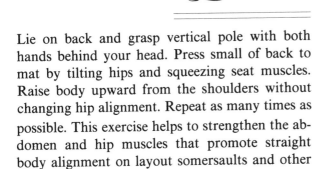

Straight Body Raise

Lie on back and grasp vertical pole with both hands behind your head. Press small of back to mat by tilting hips and squeezing seat muscles. Raise body upward from the shoulders without changing hip alignment. Repeat as many times as possible. This exercise helps to strengthen the abdomen and hip muscles that promote straight body alignment on layout somersaults and other straight body skills.

# Handstand Lower to Front (Hip Alignment Drill)

Handstand Lower to Front

This drill teaches the performer to maintain correct hip alignment while moving through a specific range of motion.

Assume a straight body handstand position. Your partner lowers you smoothly to the mat and back to a handstand while you maintain a tight hip position. Try three or four of these at the end of each workout.

## Handstand Lower to Back (Hip Alignment Drill)

This drill teaches hip alignment control while moving through a specific range of motion.

Assume a straight body handstand position. Your partner lowers you slowly to the mat and back to a handstand while you maintain a tight hip position. Try three or four at the end of each workout.

Handstand Lower to Back

# Basic Positions and Movements

Many coaches experience difficulty *introducing* tumbling to beginners. Usually, the first skill taught is a forward roll, and soon after, instruction moves to the backward roll, cartwheel, and forward handspring. But without any work on basic body position, strength, and movement, beginners can't even begin to perform some of the positions expected of them.

The reasons for teaching basic position and movements to beginners are:

1. The beginner learns basic gymnastics positions as a prerequisite to tumbling.
2. The beginner learns basic movement patterns and timing as a prerequisite to tumbling.
3. The beginner is strengthened for more advanced skills.
4. The beginner learns the basic terminology of gymnastics.
5. The movements function as additional warmup exercises.

The movements I present are only a fraction of those that an inventive instructor may introduce. Coaches often forget that virtually any movement, no matter how simple, can be a chal-

77

lenge to some beginners. A good example is the skip-step hurdle that precedes a roundoff or forward handspring. This simple hop on one foot is often not taught until the performer has learned more advanced skills. The instructor then must go back to basics and teach a skip step. Other basic techniques often overlooked include bending the hips and knees for landings, assuming a tight tucked position, and coordinating arm lift with jumping. By teaching the basic positions and movements first, a coach gives the pre-tumbler the necessary skills for smoother advancement in the sport.

## STRAIGHT BODY REST

Rest on your back with your arms held to your sides. Turn your hips under so your lower back gently presses against the mat. (Squeezing your seat muscles together helps to achieve this position.) Slowly raise your arms upward, past your chest, to a backward overhead position while keeping body straight. Note that because of structural differences, not every performer will be able to place his or her lower back flat on the mat. Do the best you can.

Straight Body Rest

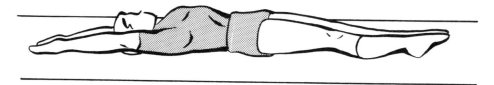

## STRAIGHT JUMP

Stand with arms held rearward. Swing arms downward, then forward and upward into a high straight body jump. As your feet leave the mat, your hips should be tucked under, your stomach held in, and your seat muscles squeezing. Land with knees slightly bent.

Straight Jump

# ARCHED REST

Lie facedown with your arms held forward. Pull stomach in, squeeze seat muscles together, and raise upper and lower body into an arched position. The tight hip position will restrict your ability to arch fully, but it will be a stable arched position.

Arched Rest

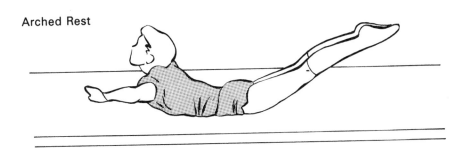

## ARCHED JUMP

Jump upward with the same arched back and tight hips as in the arched rest. Land with knees slightly bent.

Arched Jump

## TUCKED ROLLING

Sit on mat in tucked position. Grasp legs just below the knees with each hand. Roll backward to head. Push backward against mat with head and roll forward to sitting tucked position. Learn to roll forward hard enough to finish on feet with hands still holding legs.

Tucked Rolling

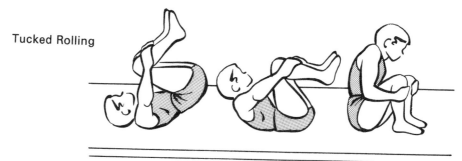

# TUCKED JUMP

Jump upward with strong arm lift. Bring bent knees upward to chest and arms downward to grasp legs. Quickly release grasp and extend legs and hips. Finish standing with slightly bent knees.

Tucked Jump

# PIKED SIT

Sit on mat with straight legs. Keeping knees straight, bend forward to your lowest piked position.

Piked Sit

Piked Jump

## PIKED JUMP

Stand with arms overhead. Swing arms downward and bend knees. Jump as arms pass hips and continue their swing, rear-upward. Quickly, raise straight legs and lower chest into piked position. Extend hips and land with slightly bent knees. This jump introduces the beginner to the "back-lift" jump technique.

## STRADDLE SIT

Sit on mat and straddle legs as wide apart as possible. Bend forward and touch toes.

Straddle Sit

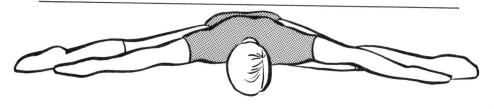

# STRADDLE JUMP

Jump with fast arm-lifting action. Quickly straddle legs and pike by bending at the waist. Touch toes. Join legs and land with slightly bent knees.

Straddle Jump

## REAR-SUPPORT ONE-HALF TURN TO FRONT SUPPORT

Sit and raise hips to rear-support position. Shift weight to one arm and turn to front-support position.

**Rear Support to Front Support**

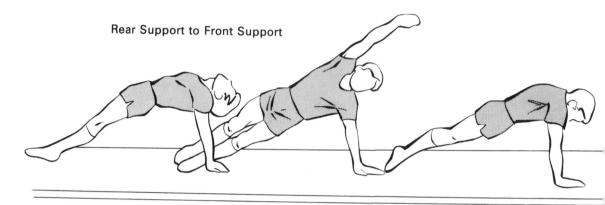

## REAR-SUPPORT FULL TURN TO REAR SUPPORT

Assume rear-support position. Shift weight to one arm and turn to front support. Keep turning in same direction to rear support.

**Rear Support to Rear Support**

# JUMP WITH ONE-HALF TURN

Jump with body straight and execute a half turn with arms held overhead. Try to keep your body as straight and as vertical as possible. Land with slightly bent knees.

Jump with One-half Turn

## JUMP WITH FULL TURN

Jump with your body straight and execute a full turn with arms held overhead. The hips should remain tight to keep the body straight throughout the turn, or landing will be awkward. This skill emphasizes the importance of the mat for initiating the twisting action. The illustration shows a forward roll into a full turn.

Jump with Full Turn

# FRONT SUPPORT AND SQUAT TO STAND

Assume a front-support position with back arched. Spring off your toes, raise
your hips with knees bent, and go into a squat stand as illustrated. You may
wish to start this series of movements from a standing position.

Front Support and Squat to Stand

# FRONT SUPPORT AND PIKE TO STAND

Assume the front-support position with your back arched. Spring off your toes,
push with arms and shoulders, and pike to stand. Finish on your feet with legs
straight and hands off the floor.

Front Support and Pike to Stand

# FRONT SUPPORT AND SQUAT TO REAR SUPPORT

Assume arched front-support position. Spring off your toes and into a squat position. Pass your legs between your arms (your hands will momentarily leave the mat), and extend your hips into the rear-support position. This action may also be performed in a piked position.

If you use your imagination, you can create other short sequences from movements described in this chapter.

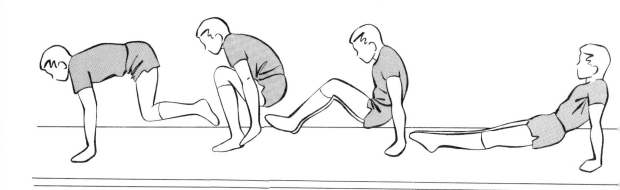

Front Support and Squat to Rear Support

# Skills
# Tumbling

## FORWARD ROLL

### Skill Level 1

The most basic forward roll starts from a low squat position with the backs of the thighs and calves touching. This illustration shows a slightly more advanced version of the forward roll starting from a semisquat position. This is generally the first forward rotating skill taught to beginners, and is a necessary prerequisite to learning the dive roll, forward salto, and other more advanced forward-rotating skills.

### Description

(1–2) Stand in a semisquat position with arms held overhead. Lean forward and place hands on the mat about shoulders' width apart.

(3–4) Push with legs and shift body weight to arms. Bend elbows and lower back of head and upper back to mat. Watch the mat until your head is about to touch. Bend knees and roll forward.

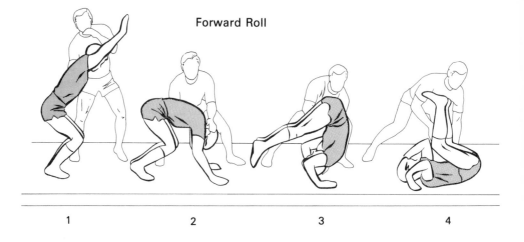

Forward Roll

1 2 3 4

(5–6) Bring upper body forward to knees until your weight is on your feet. Stand without pushing backward with your hands on the mat.

### Prerequisites

Ability to roll backward, from a squat, onto your head, and then forward to your feet.

### Spotting

(1–4) Guide the performer's head and support the neck area as he or she bends both arms for the roll. Guide the performer's legs with your other hand.
(5–6) Guide the performer to a stand by supporting the lower back.

You may also spot this roll by guiding the hips with both hands as the performer rolls over.

## STRADDLE STAND TO FORWARD ROLL TO STRADDLE STAND (VARIATION)

### Skill Level 1

The starting and finishing position of this move may be varied in numerous ways. You may start from a step, squat, straddle stand, or jump. You can finish

5         6

in a stepout, a squat, a straddle stand, a single-knee support, or a quarter turn to both knees. It is a good idea for the beginner to learn all of the variations.

## Description

(1–2) Straddle legs and place hands a shoulders' width apart on the mat. Bend elbows and lower to back of head and upper back. This illustration shows the performer in the process of straddle standing from a straddle roll and continuing into another straddle roll.

(3–4) Bring upper body forward and place hands on the mat between legs. Push with arms and finish in a straddle stand.

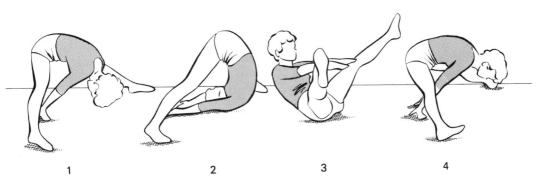

1       2       3       4

Forward Roll to Straddle Stand

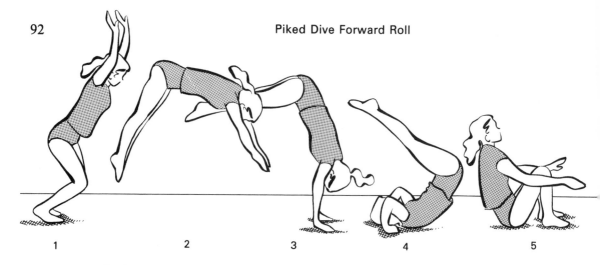

1     2     3     4     5

## PIKED DIVE ROLL (VARIATION)

## Skill Level 1

### Description

(1–3) Stand or execute a slow run. Jump with slight forward lean. You may use an over-lift (see illustration), under-lift, or backward-lift arm-thrusting technique. Bend at the waist and reach for the mat. As your hands touch, keep your eyes on the mat between them.

(4–5) Bend elbows with control and lower back of head and upper back to mat. Roll forward to a stand.

Layout Dive Forward Roll

1     2     3     4

## Prerequisites

Controlled forward roll from a small jump.

## Spotting

The spotter may support the stomach and thigh area up to the roll. The performer should learn this roll on soft mats.

# LAYOUT DIVE ROLL

## Skill Level 3

The layout dive roll may be performed with a straight or an arched body position. By itself, the arched body position is very pleasing to the eye. However, it is not functional if the performer wishes to twist with the dive, since twisting is best executed with the body held straight.

## Description

(1–4) Execute a fast run and jump. Any of the arm lifts described earlier may be used for the jump. Hold upper body fairly erect and bring lower body rear-upward to a straight or an arched body position.

(5–7) Stretch shoulders and reach for the mat. Your body will pike slightly before your hands touch the mat. Bend elbows with control, and guide the back of head and upper back to the mat. Watch the mat until you must duck your head to keep it from hitting.

(8–9) Round your back and roll to a stand.

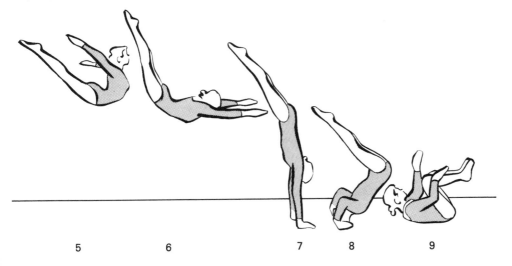

5          6               7     8          9

**Prerequisites**

Forward roll and piked dive roll.

**Spotting**

Reach under performer's stomach and thighs just after takeoff. Support and guide the performer through the roll. Practice this roll on very soft mats.

# FULL-TWISTING DIVE ROLL

## Skill Level 6

This skill was first demonstrated around 1965 in the American collegiate championships. The Europeans and Japanese started including this skill in their floor exercise routines about 1970. Eventually it was performed from handsprings and a roundoff which added considerable difficulty.

### Description

(1) Run and jump with an under-lift arm thrust. You may, however, execute this skill with either of the standard arm thrusts. Your arms should be held wider than shoulders' width apart at takeoff to allow a margin for wrapping the twist. Turn the arms and shoulders slightly as the jump occurs. Watch the mat for orientation and alignment with takeoff.

(2) Wrap the twist by quickly placing your right arm overhead and your left arm across your chest. Both arms are brought in close alignment with the longitudinal axis of rotation. You should also note that by dropping the left arm, the left side of the body is shortened, which results in right turning action. Remember, shortening one side of a forward rotating body results in an asymmetrical shape whereby the shorter side moves more quickly, which turns the body in the opposite direction. Thus, this skill employs three twisting principles: (1) initiating a small amount of twist from the floor at take-off, (2) extending the hip from a slightly piked position (body extension method) and (3) shortening one side of the body (asymmetrical radius of rotation method).

(3–4) Turn your head in the direction of the twist and be sure your body is held straight. Arching or piking will retard twisting. Look for the landing area before your hands come in contact with the mat. Reach for the mat with both arms.

(5–6) Bend your arms with control and guide your body into a forward roll.

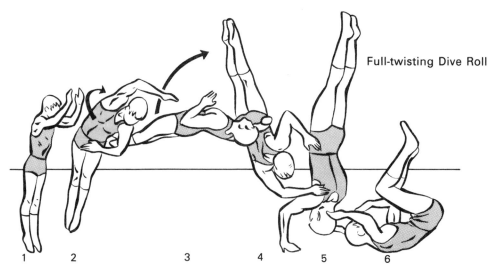

1    2    3    4    5    6

## Prerequisites

Straight-body dive roll and a jump with a full twist to a front drop on high soft mats. Some performers have learned this skill by learning to underrotate a full twisting forward salto to a back landing.

## Spotting

This skill is best spotted in an overhead safety belt. A high "catching mat" may also be used to support the performer, as illustrated.

Hand-spot by having the performer twist into you. After the first half twist, support his or her back with one hand at the hips, and roll the performer into the second half twist by grasping the other side of the hip with your other hand. Guide the performer into the roll.

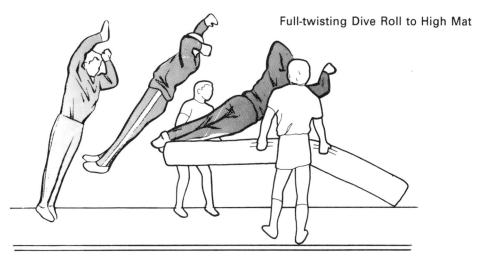

Full-twisting Dive Roll to High Mat

1 2 3 4 5 6 7 8 9 10 11

# FORWARD HANDSPRING INTO FULL-TWISTING DIVE ROLL (VARIATION)

## Skill Level 7

### Description

(1–5) See section on forward handspring. The handspring must be strong enough to land the performer in a near-standing position in immediate readiness for the jump. Any time lag between landing and takeoff can cause the jump to be ineffective.

(6–11) The overhead arm thrust must be used when working out of a forward handspring. The other arm lifts would cause an unnecessary delay in jumping.

### Prerequisites
Forward handspring to straight body dive roll and a full-twisting dive roll from a run.

### Spotting
See Full-twisting Dive Roll (page 94).

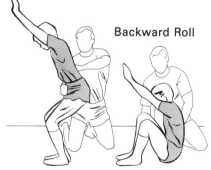

Backward Roll

1      2

# BACKWARD ROLL

## Skill Level 1

### Description

(1–3) Stand with arms held overhead. Squat to a sit and roll backward with knees close to chest. Place hands on mat below shoulders.

(4–5) Continue rolling over backward. As body weight is shifted to the back of the head, push with arms and continue rolling over to feet.

### Prerequisites
Roll on back and practice placing hands under shoulders before attempting a complete backward roll.

### Spotting
Lift and guide the performer's hips as his or her legs pass overhead.

|     |     |     |
| --- | --- | --- |
| 3   | 4   | 5   |

# PIKED SIT TO BACKWARD ROLL TO PIKED STAND (VARIATION)

## Skill Level 1

You may start a backward roll from a squat, a stride, or a piked sit, or with legs straddled. You may finish by squatting, pike standing, stepping out, straddling, or placing one knee on the mat. This illustration is just one example of several possible variations. Follow the description for the backward roll with each variation.

## Description

(1–2) Stand with arms overhead. Bend at the waist and lean backward with seat. Reach for the mat behind thighs so hands offer support before seat hits the mat.

(3–4) Roll backward and maintain piked position. Place hands on mat below shoulders. As weight shifts to head, push with arms.

Backward Roll to Piked Stand

(5–6) Hook toes (i.e. flex ankles) to grip mat, and continue pushing with arms until standing.

## Prerequisites
Backward roll from squat position and a fair degree of flexibility in a piked position.

## Spotting
See backward roll from a squat position.

5

6

**BACKWARD ROLL SHOOT TO MOMENTARY HANDSTAND**

## Skill Level 2

### Description

(1–3) Stand with arms overhead. Lean backward and squat to sit. Continue rolling and place hands on mat under shoulders. This is a fast rolling action so hands must move quickly.

(4–5) As weight shifts from lower back to shoulders, and the knees move above the face, shoot legs upward by forcefully extending hips. At the same time, push with arms and finish in a straight body handstand.

### Prerequisites
Backward roll to squat stand. Practice shooting legs on your back from a resting piked position with spotter pulling you up to a handstand.

### Spotting
Grasp performer's legs at the knees as he or she shoots upward. Pull forcefully upward into a handstand.

Backward Roll Shoot to Momentary Handstand

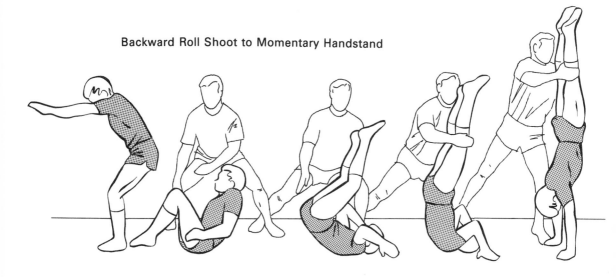

1     2     3     4     5

# BACKWARD ROLL SHOOT TO HANDSTAND WITH ONE-HALF TURN (VARIATION)

## Skill Level 3

This skill requires a fast rolling action coupled with an aggressive leg shoot and arm push. Before attempting the illustrated "hop-turning" action, learn a half turn with support on one arm. Do this by turning the wrist of your support arm inward or outward, prior to the shoot and push, in the direction you wish to turn. As you shoot your legs upward, shift your body weight to the support arm and turn with the turn of your wrist.

Backward Roll to Handstand with One-half Turn

# CARTWHEEL

## Skill Level 2

The cartwheel is probably the first kicking skill you'll learn as a beginner. The first leg you kick over your head must coordinate with the hand you wish to place first on the mat. If you wish to kick your *right leg* over your head, your *left hand* must be the first hand to touch the mat. You can decide on your best kicking leg by practicing a couple of kicks to a handstand with a spotter catching your kicking leg for stability. The leg that you feel gives you the best kicking power is the leg that you should use on *all* kicking skills. The illustration shows a performer who feels most comfortable kicking his right leg over his head. Therefore, he places his left hand first on the mat. Do not base your choice of which kicking leg to use on whether you are right- or left-handed. That formula just doesn't work. There are some people who feel equally as efficient kicking either leg. If that's the case with you, base your decision on which side you feel best turning to as you bend to perform a cartwheel. If you decide to kick your right leg over your head, *all* your future skip-step hurdles will be executed by hopping on your right foot and then stepping forward onto your left. See Hurdles (page 36) if you have any questions about this procedure.

Cartwheel

1    2    3

## Description

(1–3) To do a cartwheel, stand sideways with arms held obliquely overhead. Raise your left leg sideward with your hips turned slightly to the left. Step and lean to the left. Bend your left knee. Place your left hand on the mat (fingers facing left) and kick your right leg over your head.

(4–6) Place your right hand on the mat (fingers facing left), in front of your left hand, and pass through a handstand with your legs held as far apart as possible. Stretch upward through your shoulders and watch the mat between your hands. Place your right leg on the mat close to your right hand. Stand with arms held obliquely overhead.

## Prerequisites

Some experience kicking up to handstand position. A fair degree of hip and leg flexibility.

## Spotting

(1–3) Stand to the rear of the performer. Place your right hand, palm up, on stomach and hip area. As performer bends sideward, grasp hip on other side and guide performer up to handstand.

(4–6) Gently pull upward and guide performer through handstand. As performer steps to right leg, lift and support right side of hip with your left hand.

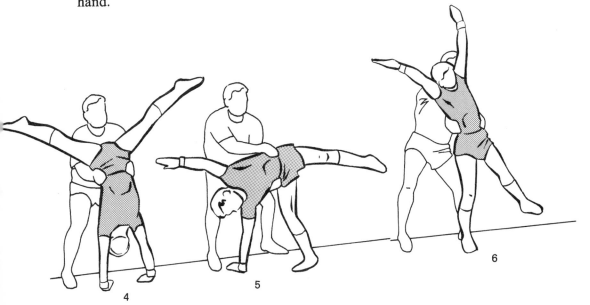

4      5      6

Dive Cartwheel

## DIVE CARTWHEEL (VARIATION)

### Skill Level 3

Execute a skip step from a short run with arms lifting forward and upward (under lift). Push off forward leg and kick rear leg into diving cartwheel. Attempt to gain as much elevation as possible before hands touch for cartwheel. This is done by decreasing the amount of forward lean at takeoff. As your first hand touches the mat, your body should be moving through a straddled handstand position with a smooth rolling action.

Some coaches teach the diving action from one step before progressing to the skip-step stage. It often helps to have the performer practice diving over low rolled mats to get the feeling of lifting before touching. A spotter may help the performer lift at takeoff by lightly raising the hips.

## ROUNDOFF

### Skill Level 2

The roundoff is one of the most important skills in tumbling. It is the means by which every tumbler turns in preparation for a backward tumbling series. As with the hurdle into the roundoff, the roundoff should be a powerful extension of the run. If it is executed short and high, without the lean that establishes

linear distance, a loss of speed will result. The length of the roundoff must always be in relation to the speed of the run.

Many beginners have difficulty with this skill because they attempt to turn too much during the first half of it. This action usually delays the placement of the second support hand on the mat, which weakens (mis-times) the arm thrust. Instead, the tumbler should be taught to reach for the mat with the second hand so the body weight can be shifted to both arms at an earlier period in the skill. In order to avoid this common problem, many coaches will instruct their beginners to watch the first arm during the first phase, thus eliminating premature turning of the head which tends to promote late placement of the second hand on the mat.

## Description

(1–2) Stand facing straight down the mat with arms overhead. Raise the left leg and lean forward. Step onto the left leg and bend knee about halfway. At the same time, bend forward at the waist and reach for the mat with your arms.

(3–4) Place left hand (fingers facing left) on the mat and kick right leg overhead by pushing with left leg. Place right hand on the mat, in front of left hand, with fingers facing left. The right hand is turned slightly more than the left hand and is placed on the mat a couple of inches to the left of the left hand (see illustration). As the legs come together overhead, your body weight shifts from one to both arms. Your eyes

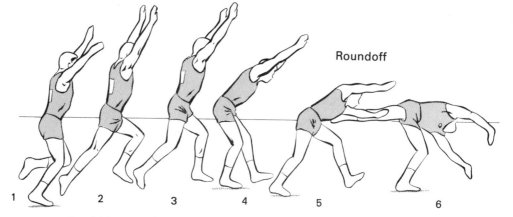

Roundoff

should be watching the mat between your hands at all times.

(5–12) As your legs join, the second quarter turn is then completed with a forceful push off both arms, and your hips are bent (piked). The motion should be continuous from kick to landing. Upon landing, both arms should be extended in front of you in a symmetrical position. Your feet should be placed under your hips and your knees should be very slightly bent in preparation for a jump.

## Prerequisites

A fast cartwheel with good control.

## Spotting

(1–4) Stand to the left of the performer if he or she is to perform a left-hand-down-first roundoff. Grasp the performer's hips as if to spot a cartwheel.

(5) As the performer's legs join, turn his or her hips so the stomach faces the mat upon landing.

Spotting the Roundoff

7      8      9    10        11        12

# HEADSPRING

## Skill Level 3

The headspring may be performed from a dive and may finish in numerous positions, including a stepout, a straddle stand, a straddle sit, or a piked sit.

## Description

(1–2) Assume a low squat position. Place your hands on the mat, about shoulders' width apart, and about twelve inches in front of knees. Bend your elbows and place your head on the mat between your hands. Push off mat with toes until your legs straighten into a deep piked position. This action should force your hips forward, over your head.

(3–6) Maintain deep piked position until you feel your hips moving slightly beyond your head-hand support. Quickly extend hips to arched position and simultaneously push against mat to straighten your arms. This ac-

4           5

## Headspring

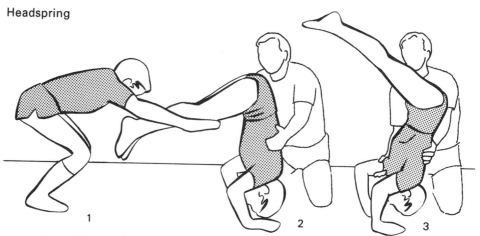

tion will provide shoulder elevation and forward rotation.

Land with your back slightly arched, arms overhead, and head held slightly back. If your arm thrust is strong, you will land on your feet. If your arm thrust is weak, you will probably finish in a bridge.

### Prerequisites

Jump to forward roll. Backward roll shoot to handstand. Standup from a bridge.

### Spotting

(1–3) Kneel at side of performer. Hold lower back and grasp upper arm.
(4–6) Support and guide performer to a stand. Maintain your grasp on the upper arm until landing occurs, so that the arm doesn't inadvertently strike you.

This skill is often taught with head and hand support on rolled or piled mats. The elevated mat surface provides additional shoulder elevation which makes a balanced landing easier.

# HEADSPRING TO TUCKED FORWARD SALTO (VARIATION)

## Skill Level 7

This sequence requires very strong hip extension and arm push during the headspring action. The performer must land standing fairly erect with enough forward motion to jump effectively into the forward salto. The headspring is almost always preceded by a jump or hurdle which adds power to the headspring. Practice the headspring into a forward dive roll before attempting to bound into a salto. See Forward Handspring to Tucked Forward Salto (page 139) for additional information.

Headspring to Tucked Forward Salto

# BACKWARD WALKOVER

## Skill Level 3

Practice kicking one leg over your head from a bridge before trying the backward walkover. This drill will teach you the kicking action and the weight-shifting action necessary for performance.

## Description

(1–2) Stand with arms overhead. Place your left foot forward so pointed toe touches the mat. Stretch upward through your stomach and chest. Lower upper body backward and press your hips forward slightly to compensate for your backward arch.

(3–4) Place your hands on the mat as close to your right leg as possible. Your right knee will now be slightly bent. Push with your right leg and raise your left leg upward toward a handstand. Watch the mat between your hands.

(5–6) Continue pulling left leg overhead so legs are forced into a near split position. Extend in the shoulders. Place your left foot on the mat and hold your right leg as high as possible as you stand.

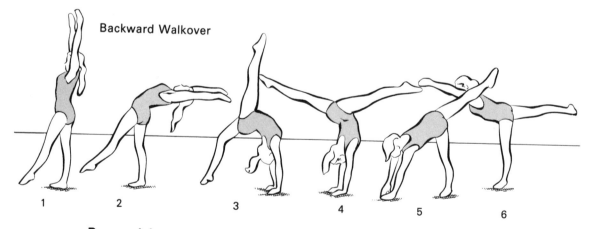

Backward Walkover

1    2    3    4    5    6

## Prerequisites

Ability to stand up from a bridge, lower to a bridge from a stand, kick through a handstand with one leg from a bridge, execute a controlled kick to handstand, and perform a fair split.

## Spotting

Stand to the forward-leg side of the performer. Place one hand on his or her lower back and your other hand under the thigh. As the performer arches backward, support the back and guide the forward leg through the handstand phase. As the performer passes through the handstand, shift the hand supporting the leg to the stomach and the hand supporting the back to the high leg. Guide the performer to a stand.

# FORWARD WALKOVER

## Skill Level 3

The forward walkover is an acrobatic skill that requires a great deal of flexibility in the split position and in the hip and shoulder areas. The beginning performer should not attempt this skill until he or she has learned to stand properly from a bridge. The forward walkover is performed with a smooth continuous motion.

## Description

(1–2) Stand with arms extended overhead. Raise your right leg forward. Step onto your right leg. Bend your right knee and place your hands on the mat slightly in front of your shoulders. Kick your left leg overhead by straightening the right knee.

(3–4) Split legs as wide apart as possible as your body passes through a handstand position. Gently press your shoulders backward as your lead leg overbalances. Watch the mat between your hands. Place your left foot on the mat as close to your hands as possible. Push off your hands and shift your body weight forward onto your left leg. Keep watching the mat between your hands.

(5) Stand by leading with your hips and stretching your right leg forward. Keep your back arched as your body weight completely shifts forward to your left leg. Do not pull your head forward as you stand because you'll round your upper back and retard your forward hip lead. When you are balanced on your left leg, raise your upper body to an erect standing position.

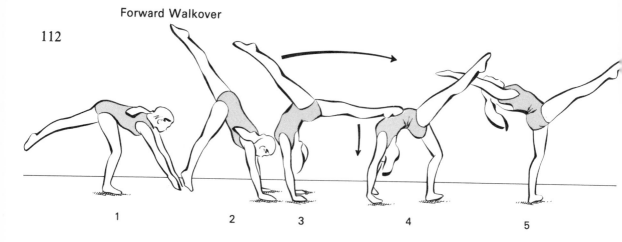

Forward Walkover

1  2  3  4  5

## Prerequisites

Standup from a bridge. Handstand arch over to bridge and stand. Fair control in handstand position. Ability to perform a split is desirable but not necessary.

## Spotting

Stand to the side of the performer. As he or she kicks through a handstand, place your hands on the lower back and stomach. Gently press the performer into position as he or she arches over. Guide the performer to a stand as he or she attempts to shift weight forward. The pressure of the spotter's hands should encourage correct position and lean.

Dive Forward Walkover

# DIVE FORWARD WALKOVER (VARIATION)

## Skill Level 4

Execute a skip step with arms lifting forward and upward or rearward and upward. The illustration shows a rear-upward lift with arms moving out to the sides early in the lift.

Leap off the mat with the upper body held in a horizontal position. Reach for the mat with your arms and execute a forward walkover. You may practice this leaping action by placing folded mats in front of you so you are forced to elevate and take some distance. Start with little leaps and build to higher elevation over a period of time.

**FORWARD HANDSPRING**

## Skill Level 4

The forward handspring is a fairly difficult skill for most beginners to learn well. The problem may be broken down into three natural negative tendencies that seem to be common during the early stages of performance.

1. The natural tendency to duck the head under, toward the chest, as the kickover is initiated. Early ducking of the head stifles optical orientation, encourages forward shoulder lean, and inhibits the kicking motion.
2. The natural tendency to lean forward with the shoulders in the direction of the movement. The forward shoulder lean will lower the body's center of gravity and inhibit arm and shoulder extension.
3. The natural tendency to pull the upper body forward in an effort to "see" the landing area. This action automatically inhibits hyperextension (arching) of the back and encourages placement of the feet in front of the hips upon landing.

Any of these negative tendencies can ruin a successful performance. The illustration deals with the last problem. The black dot, on the performer's hip, represents the center of gravity. In order to land the handspring correctly, the base of support (feet) should be placed under the center of gravity. A very powerful performer may modify this position slightly.

## Description

(1–2) Take one or two fast walking steps. Execute a skip step with a fair amount of forward lean. Step forward with your left leg and bend your knee about halfway. Place your hands on the mat about six inches *in front of your shoulders*. Forcefully extend your left knee and kick your right leg overhead. Watch the mat between your hands. Push upward with your arms so your shoulders extend completely. Continue watching the mat as your legs move overhead.

(3) Join your legs and assume an arched back position. Place your feet under your hips with both arms extended overhead.

Poor Landing

1 2 3

Forward Handspring

## Prerequisites

Ability to thrust kicking leg overhead, through a handstand, with lots of power. You may practice this against a matted wall or into the arms of a spotter. The ability to stand from a bridge is recommended, but not essential.

## Spotting

Stand to the right side of performer. As the performer's hands touch the mat, grasp his or her upper arm with your left hand and place your right hand (forearm for heavy spot) under his or her lower back. Support and guide performer to a stand.

# FORWARD HANDSPRING TO STEPOUT (VARIATION)

## Skill Level 4

The illustration shows a forward handspring stepout as performed by an Olympic finalist. Note his hand placement on the mat, in relation to his shoulders, as he initiates the kick. This extreme forward reach enables him to "block," or push against the mat, to gain elevation. The beginning performer should mainly be concerned with getting his or her first leg under the hip for the landing. See Forward Handspring (page 114).

Jump to Forward Handspring

# JUMP INTO FORWARD HANDSPRING (VARIATION)

## Skill Level 5

This skill is generally performed after a skill that provides forward motion for the jump, such as a forward handspring or a salto. The performer jumps forward into a slightly piked handstand and forcefully extends the hips into an arched back position. Then, while the hips are extending, the performer pushes with arms and shoulders to land in an arched stand.

**HANDSTAND SNAPDOWN**

## Skill Level 3

The handstand snapdown is probably the most important—and at the same time the most neglected—skill in tumbling. This action is similar to the second half of a backward handspring. It is the means by which the tumbler establishes the angle of block against the mat, the position of the body at the moment of contact with the mat, and the linear and angular force at takeoff. If the snapdown is weak, the power of the subsequent movements will diminish in direct proportion to the degree of inefficiency of the snapdown.

If the snapdown leaves the performer's upper body too low at the moment of contact with the mat, the ensuing jump will be delayed by precious moments which will inhibit elevation and rotation. The poor tumbler generally solves this problem by quickly arching backward in order to place the center of gravity over the feet at takeoff time. .

The snapping-down action teaches the tumbler to use the elastic qualities inherent in the human body. The body moves by means of internal muscle force. From the handstand position, slightly bent knees are straightened, the hip joint moves from hyperextension to flexion, the shoulder girdle moves from depression to extension, the elbows are slightly flexed and then extended, and the wrists are straightened. Without these ranges of motion the tumbler would be like a stick flopping end over end, unable to change position.

## Description

(1) To do a handstand snapdown, kick to a near handstand position. Arch your back and bend your knees slightly. Allow your shoulders to sag slightly and bend your elbows a little. Beginners should not bend their elbows unless their arms are fairly strong.

(2) Quickly straighten your knees and flex your hips. As the hips flex, push against the mat with your arms (extend shoulders and elbows). Round your back and watch the mat between your hands.

(3) Land with your feet placed below your hips and about eighteen inches from your original hand position on the mat. This distance is only approximate and varies with the size of the performer.

(4) Swing your arms upward into a jump immediately upon landing (rebound). Practice rebounding into forward, backward, and straight-up jumps.

Handstand Snapdown

1    2    3    4

## Prerequisites

Ability to assume a fairly controlled handstand position.

## Spotting

Stand to the side of the performer. Grasp his or her hips on the sides and lift the performer into a high landing position during the snapdown. The spotter should guide the performer into a pattern of elevation and rotation.

**BACKWARD HANDSPRING**

## Skill Level 5

To most beginners, the backward handspring represents the link between beginning and intermediate tumbling ability. For this reason, most beginners, in their anxiety to excel, try to learn the backward handspring prematurely.

Coaches and gymnasts should keep in mind that the backward handspring requires the physical ability to execute a strong rotating jump backward and a well-coordinated snapdown from a handstand. Perhaps more importantly, the performer is faced for the first time with the problem of "follow-through" on the jump, while simultaneously trying to rotate backwards quickly. The second problem (rotation) tends to "feel" inconsistent with the more important follow-through on the jumping phase. This dilemma is similar to the beginning diver who, so concerned with rotating forward to a hands-first entry, overleans and loses the push off the diving board.

The "look" of a backward handspring is also confusing to beginners. To the untrained eye, it appears to be a single, fast, turning-over-backward motion, with the hands touching the mat. Beginners seldom analyze it as a two-phase skill that gains impetus from changing the body shape from an arch to a pike during the hand-push phase. Let's break it down into its three basic components as prerequisites to learning the complete skill.

First, the beginner should be taught how to jump backward for distance. This can be accomplished by jumping backward to a sitting position onto soft hip level mats. Second, the beginner must experience orientation while turning

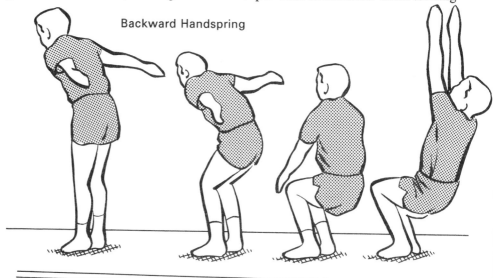

Backward Handspring

1          2          3          4

over backward. This can be taught by means of slow-motion drills whereby the performer is carried through a mock backward handspring. Third, the beginner must learn the handstand snapdown phase (see Handstand Snapdown, page 70). Finally, after he or she can do each well, the beginner should put the components all together either with the aid of a safety belt or a good hand spot.

A backward handspring may be executed with a kick into it (gainer), a step out of it, a half turn off the hands, or with a full twist.

## Description

(1–2) Stand with your arms held high to the rear of your hips. Bend your knees and initiate a slight backward lean. *Do not allow your upper body to drop.*

(3–4) Drive your arms forward and upward. During this phase, your knees continue bending until your thighs are parallel with the floor. The backward lean is smoothly increased as your upper body stretches upward with your arms leading. Push forcefully with your legs against the mat.

(5–6) As you arch your back and reach for the mat with your hands, continue pushing with your legs, right to the tips of your toes. As your hands touch the mat your back should be arched. Most likely your knees will be slightly bent, which will enhance the ensuing snapdown. Do not consciously try to bend them. The kneebend tends to happen naturally. Beginners should not bend their arms as the illustration shows. The strong advanced performer has the ability to forcefully straighten his or her arms in order to further increase the power of the snapdown.

(7–8) As your hips pass over your head, push against the mat with your arms

5　　　　　　6　　　　　7　　　　　8

and pike down sharply. A forceful push off the mat with "follow-through" will generally cause your upper back to round (concave chest), your head to lower between your arms, your shoulders to extend, and your arms to straighten.

The illustration shows an Olympic bronze-medal floor-exercise champion performing a standing backward handspring that leads into a series of four more backward handsprings. This accounts for his knees never quite straightening during the snapdown; he was preparing for the next leg push into another handspring.

### Prerequisites
Fairly controlled handstand. Handstand snapdown. Experience in most forward springing skills. See introduction to Backward Handspring.

Spotting the Backward Handspring

1          2                    3                    4

(1–3) Kneel at the performer's side and place your hand or entire arm (heavy spot) under his or her lower back. Place your other hand under the thigh. Guide the performer's bend and lean motion with the hand on his or her back.

(4–5) Assist the performer's jump and arch by supporting his or her lower back. Aid rotation by lifting the thigh upward after the jump off the mat. Carefully place performer in a snapdown position. Weak performers may allow their arms to buckle as their hands contact the mat. *Beware.*

(6–9) Guide the performer into a snapdown.

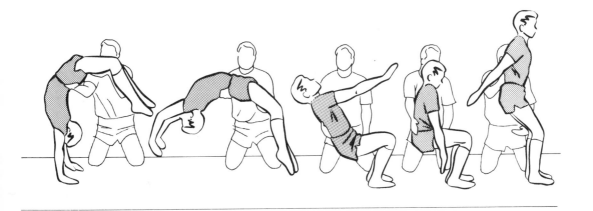

| 5 | 6 | 7 | 8 | 9 |

# BACKWARD HANDSPRING WITH ONE-HALF TWIST (VARIATION)

## Skill Level 5

This skill requires a forceful snapdown action along with a hip turn in the direction of the twist. As you can see from the illustration, the shoulders must elevate throughout the second phase in order to arrive in a high, standing position. The snapdown and hip-turn action may be learned on an elevated surface (mat pile) before adding it to the handspring.

Backward Handspring with One-half Twist

# BACKWARD HANDSPRING WITH FULL TWIST TO FRONT SUPPORT (VARIATION)

## Skill Level 6

This skill may be learned by performing a back-dive one-half twist to a handstand and then adding a roundoff hand placement before the hands touch the mat. First, learn to jump to a handstand with a half twist on soft mats. Then add a roundoff before the hands touch the mat. Notice that in order to make this skill a full twist in *one* direction, the performer executes a half turn to the right and then puts his or her left hand down first for the roundoff action.

## Spotting

Spot from the side and have the performer twist into you. Support his or her
stomach with your right arm and grasp the waist, from over the back, with your
left hand. Pull him or her through the left-hand-down-first roundoff with lots
of support. If the roundoff must be performed contrary to the performer's
normal direction, he or she must practice roundoffs on the unnatural side before
attempting this skill. Of course, the performer has the option of changing the
direction of the initial twist, but this tends to be more difficult for most gymnasts since it is inconsistent with their direction on similar but more difficult
skills (see Which Direction Should I Learn to Twist?, page 52).

# BACKWARD HANDSPRING WITH A FULL TWIST TO A STEPOUT (VARIATION)

## Skill Level 6

This skill may be performed from a stand, a cartwheel, a backward handspring, or a roundoff. The full twist in the illustration stemmed from a roundoff action that finished in a stepout position. The performer pushes off both feet simultaneously and dives high for the full twist. He or she watches the mat for the entire skill after the initial half twist is completed. The performer must learn to retard backward rotation by jumping almost straight up. This is particularly difficult if he or she has already mastered the backward salto with a full twist, which requires a hard thrust backward for rotation.

### Spotting
See Backward Handspring with a Full Twist to a Front Support (page 124) for some spotting hints.

## Skill Level 5

These skills are generally the first combination of backward tumbling movements that the intermediate performer learns. Some performers learn this series before being able to execute a backward handspring from a stand, although this is not recommended by many coaches. A standing backward handspring requires a fair amount of leg pushing power, which many young gymnasts don't have. Thus, coach and gymnast often bypass the standing handspring by substituting the speed from a roundoff to compensate for lack of leg power. Although this approach has some merit, it is inconsistent with the theory of progressions.

## Description

(1–3) Execute a roundoff from one or two fast steps and a hurdle. Attempt to kick your first leg overhead and directly to the mat on the other side with one continuous motion. The other leg should follow with equally continuous motion. The legs should not slow as they pass overhead. As your legs pass through the handstand position, push with your arms and extend your shoulders in order to gain upper-body elevation.

(4–5) Place your feet on the mat under your hips. Sometimes it helps to watch your feet as they land. Upon landing, bend your knees and lean backward with your hips. Throw your *arms* and upper body backward. If your arm push off the mat is weak, you will have difficulty placing your feet under your hips; poor backward lean may result. This failure is characterized by an excessively high backward handspring.

(6–7) Quickly reach for the mat with your hands in order to assume a momentary handstand with your back arched. Snapdown to your feet by flexing your hips and pushing away from the mat with your arms.

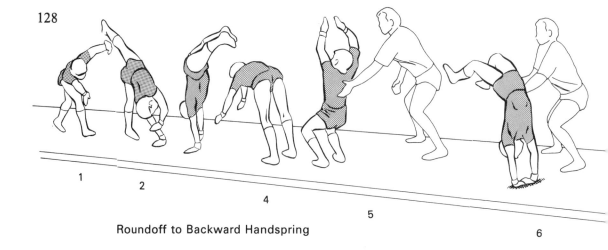

**Roundoff to Backward Handspring**

1  2  4  5  6

## Prerequisites

Roundoff with fair power. A standing backward handspring is recommended.

## Spotting

Use an overhead safety belt if you have one. Hand-spot by standing well ahead of the performer. Anticipate the landing area after the roundoff. Place your hand (forearm for heavy spot) under the performer's lower back. Guide the performer through the handstand and on to his or her feet. A word of caution: The beginner may quit in the middle of the performance until he or she has gained confidence. The spotter must move wherever the performer moves and be prepared for trouble.

Snapdown to Backward Handspring

7

# SNAPDOWN TO BACKWARD HANDSPRING DRILL (VARIATION)

## Skill Level 5

This drill places emphasis on snapdown action, and teaches foot placement and lean to increase power.

The spotter may assist the snapdown action and follow the performer with a lower-back spot throughout the series. If you are a serious tumbler and can do a backward handspring, you should learn and practice this sequence often.

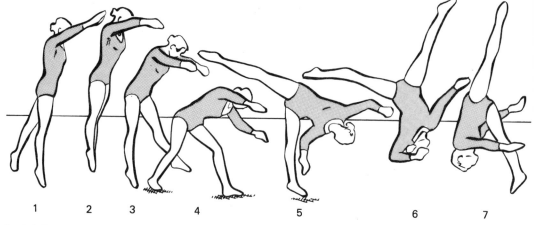

1  2  3  4  5  6  7

Aerial Cartwheel

# AERIAL CARTWHEEL

## Skill Level 5

This skill requires a strong leg kick and a fair amount of leg flexibility in the split position. It should be learned from a skip step and eventually from a stand if it is to be used in floor exercise.

## Description

(1–4) Execute one or two walking steps and a hurdle with your arms overhead. Step forward with your lead foot slightly in front of your shoulders as you bend forward. Bend your lead knee (right angle or slightly less) as your arms swing forward and down.

(5–10) Kick your back leg overhead and push with your forward leg as your arms lift backward and sideward. Your arm lift should be coordinated with your leg push. Turn your head and shoulders in the direction of the twist and watch the mat area just in front of your forward leg. As your legs pass through a straddled handstand position, pull the lead leg under you by flexing your hip. Your lead leg should land on the mat directly under your hips. Your legs should also be far apart when you land. If they aren't, you're probably allowing your lead leg to slow down as it passes overhead.

## Prerequisites

Cartwheel. Roundoff. One-arm cartwheel. Forward handspring stepout. The ability to perform a split also helps.

8    9    10

## Spotting

See Cartwheel (page 102). Many coaches teach this skill by requiring the performer to execute a far- or near-arm one-arm cartwheel, with little or no weight on the support arm. This action helps the performer get the "feeling" of kicking up and over the support arm. Eventually, the performer learns to keep the support hand away from the mat.

# AERIAL BARANI (VARIATION)

## Skill Level 5

The aerial barani requires a bit more power in the initial kicking action than an aerial cartwheel. As the pushing leg leaves the mat, both legs are quickly joined for the landing.

Aerial Barani

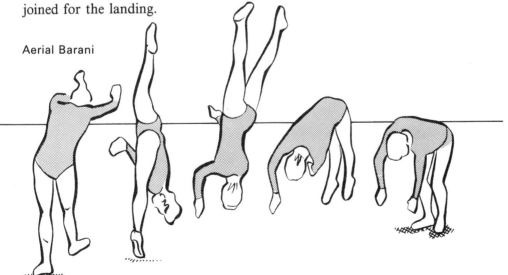

Aerial Walkover

# AERIAL WALKOVER

## Skill Level 6

This skill requires more flexibility in the hip and lower back areas than the aerial cartwheel does. The landing is also more difficult because the performer cannot easily watch the mat during the salto and landing. Most beginners make the mistake of ducking their heads forward, in the middle of the performance, in an attempt to "see" where they are going. This action causes an inadequate arch, which inhibits placement of the first-landing leg under the hips at landing. The beginner should learn to watch the mat until the kicking leg lands.

## Description

(1–3) Take one or two walking steps into a hurdle. Step forward with your left foot slightly in front of your shoulders as your upper body bends forward. The arms move forward and down.

(4–7) Kick your right leg overhead by pushing off the mat with your left leg until it is straight. Arms move rearward and then out to the side. The arms and shoulders "lift" as the kick occurs. Watch the mat as your legs pass through the inverted position. The kicking leg should move, non-stop, directly to the mat on the other side. A very flexible performer can

6          7

actually watch his or her first foot land on the mat. Place your right foot on the mat under your hips, and hold your head backward. Continue arching up to a stand.

## Prerequisites

The flexibility of a forward walkover and the kicking power of a forward handspring.

## Spotting

Stand to the side of performer. Place your closest hand on the stomach as he or she bends forward. Place your other hand on the lower back after he or she kicks. Support and guide performer to a stand.

Spotting the Aerial Walkover

**FORWARD SALTO**

## Skill Level 6

See The Importance of Prerequisites (page 55), which outlines one fairly complete method commonly used to teach the forward salto. Along with the section on prerequisites, the reader should review Arm Lift on Forward Salto Skills (page 39).

Forward Salto to High Mats

The most effective and advanced arm-lift technique for executing a single forward salto is the back lift. This method of arm lift is generally taught after the other more common methods have been mastered. Besides knowing the prerequisites, using a high pile of landing mats seems to improve the back-lift forward-salto technique very quickly. Beginning performers using this arm-lift technique often tend to throw the upper portion of their bodies downward at the moment of takeoff. Practicing with high piled mats necessitates a fairly erect takeoff. Indeed, the high-mat method helps when practicing any arm-lifting action, but particularly the back-lift-style salto.

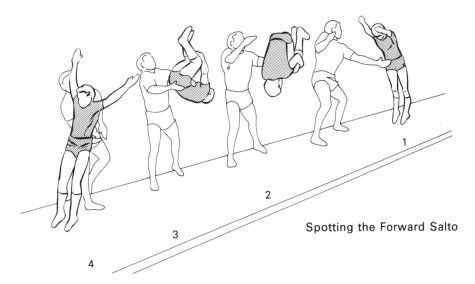

Spotting the Forward Salto

## Description

(1–2) Take three or four running steps and execute a low, short hurdle. Your hurdle should be an extension of your running pattern rather than a high leap from a one- to a two-foot landing.

The demonstrator in the illustration uses an under-lift arm action. The arms swing past the hips, from the rear, lifting forward and upward as the jump occurs.

The feet are placed slightly in front of the hips prior to the jump. This slight blocking action is proportionate to the speed of the run. A fast run and hurdle requires more block, which translates to greater elevation.

Spring upward and very slightly forward off your legs without lowering your upper body. At this moment, your back should be rounded (chest concave) and your chin pressed inward toward your neck. You establish your pattern of forward rotation by leaning slightly forward as you jump.

Quickly, round your back and grasp your knees in a tight tucked position. This action speeds up the rotation you've established from your initial straight-body jump off the floor. If you didn't tuck, you'd probably have only enough forward rotation for a high dive roll.

(3–4) Hold the tucked position until you "feel" yourself rotating to a standing position. Attempt to see some portion of the gym in front of you for optical orientation. Land with your feet more or less under your hips. The timing of your release from the tucked position will determine where your feet land. Always land with your hips and knees slightly bent to absorb the shock of landing.

### Prerequisites
See The Importantance of Prerequisites (page 55).

### Spotting
Stand to the side of the performer. Place your near hand on the performer's stomach at takeoff. Lift and support. Support the performer's hips or lower back with your other hand, as he or she rotates forward. Continue holding the performer up until the landing.

# FORWARD SALTO TO STEPOUT WITH UNDER-LIFT ARM ACTION (VARIATION)

## Skill Level 6

The stepout technique is used to move directly into a skill that requires a single-leg takeoff, such as a roundoff or forward handspring.

This forward salto must be executed with slightly more rotation because the earlier extension of the hips and knees retards rotation. The first stepout foot should land under the hips, with a slight bend in the knee and hip joints. The performer should know how to overrotate and jump out of a regular forward salto before attempting the stepout.

Forward Salto to Stepout with Under-lift
Arm Action

# FORWARD SALTO TO STEPOUT WITH OVER-LIFT ARM ACTION (VARIATION)

## Skill Level 6

This illustration demonstrates the basic arm lift that most beginners are taught, as performed by an N.C.A.A. floor-exercise finalist. Refer to Arm Lift on Forward Salto Skills (page 39) for more information.

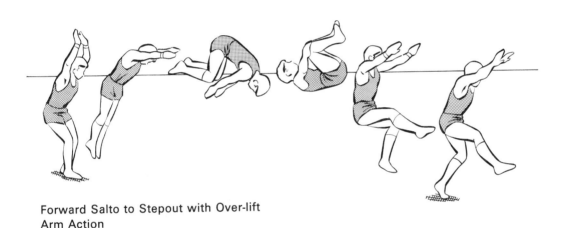

Forward Salto to Stepout with Over-lift
Arm Action

# FORWARD ONE-AND-ONE-QUARTER SALTO TO FRONT SUPPORT (VARIATION)

## Skill Level 7

This illustration shows a World Games finalist using back-lift arm action to go into an "overrotated" forward salto. This skill may be learned by jumping from a vaulting board into a crash mat. The performer's feet touch the floor momentarily prior to hand contact with the mat. The arms are quickly flexed somewhat to absorb the shock of impact.

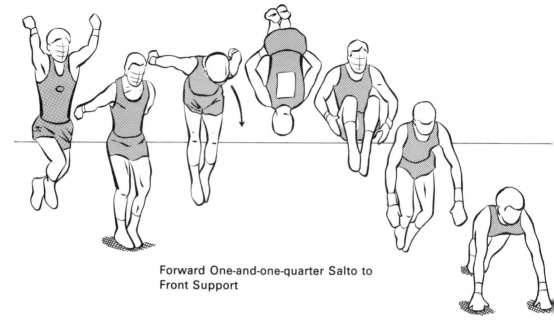

Forward One-and-one-quarter Salto to
Front Support

# FORWARD SALTO FROM BACKWARD SALTO (VARIATION)

## Skill Level 9

This skill may be performed from a tucked layout or twisting salto. It is particularly difficult because you must be strong enough to change your direction of rotation immediately upon landing. In the illustration, the performer's feet are placed behind his hips, at an extreme blocking angle that clearly demonstrates the high degree of force required to reverse linear and rotary motion.

Forward Salto from Backward Salto

To do this skill, you must first learn a forward salto from a jump in place, then from a jump backward. Knowing how far you've rotated backward is crucial to the angle of foot placement at takeoff for the forward phase of the skill. The overhead safety belt or a good hand-spot may be used after you've mastered the initial jump to salto. The Achilles tendon (the large tendon that attaches to the heel) is extremely vulnerable in a change of direction skill such as this. Be sure you stretch and warm up your ankles well, before each training session.

# FORWARD HANDSPRING TO TUCKED FORWARD SALTO (VARIATION)

## Skill Level 7

The most critical phase of this skill combination is the landing and jumping phase. Both coach and performer will often become frustrated with the jump from what may seem an excellent forward handspring.

Generally speaking, the problem arises due to the structural limitations of the human body. Consider, for example, a backward handspring to a backward salto. In this instance, the performer, after landing on his or her hands during the backward handspring, snaps down by flexing the hips and extending the

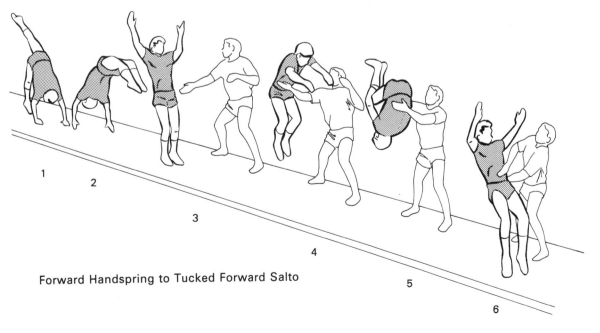

Forward Handspring to Tucked Forward Salto

1  2  3  4  5  6

knees through a substantial and powerful range of motion. The snapdown also affords very clear kinesthetic orientation for powerful shoulder girdle and arm extension. These factors allow a great range for body placement and for error. As the snapdown performer jumps into the backward salto, the arms, hips, and knees are advantageously positioned for a jump.

By comparison, the structural limitations of the forward handspring "tighten" the range of acceptable performance for jumping. Joining the legs in an arched position, after the initial kick, is a substantially weaker action than snapping down into a pike. The range of motion is smaller (arching as opposed to piking), and the hip and lower back muscles can barely be used. Arm and shoulder extension during the forward handspring is also less effective, because it occurs obliquely at the beginning of the skill. Thus, attractive as the forward handspring may appear, the performer attempting it often can't land with his or her feet under the body, in the correct position to jump.

The forward handspring should be executed low and fast with lots of arm push and *complete* shoulder extension as your feet pass over your head. You should land for the jump with your body almost straight. The weaker your handspring, the more balanced you must land. As you land, your ankles, knees, and hips should be slightly flexed, your shoulders depressed, and your elbows slightly bent. Now your body is ready to extend into a jump.

Jump forward and upward with your hips slightly in front of your feet, then quickly tuck as tightly as possible. Refer to Forward Salto (page 134) for more information.

## Spotting

Spot by standing to the side and well ahead of the performer. As the performer completes the handspring (1–3), place your near hand (forearm for heavy spot) on his or her stomach (4). Support performer. As the performer ducks his or her head, reach over the back and support the lower back (5). Rotate performer by pushing with your arms in the direction of rotation (6).

# FORWARD HANDSPRING TO PIKED FORWARD SALTO (VARIATION)

## Skill Level 7

Most well-executed piked forward saltos are characterized by a tightly piked position and complete body extension prior to landing. Although they needn't, most performers grasp the back of the upper legs to insure a tight pike for faster rotation. Many coaches advocate practicing a layed-out salto, in an overhead belt or a foam pit, in order to overemphasize hip thrust at takeoff. Although this teaching technique reverses normal learning sequence, the results are often quite beneficial.

Forward Handspring to Piked Forward Salto

# FORWARD HANDSPRING TO PIKED FORWARD SALTO TO STEPOUT (VARIATION)

## Skill Level 7

The piked forward salto requires a substantially stronger forward handspring than a tucked salto. The illustration shows an Olympic champion landing from her handspring in a fairly arched position that increases her range of motion for thrusting forward into a pike after the jump. While piking, she shortens her radius of rotation by ducking her head and bringing her arms downward toward her hips. When her back is approximately parallel to the floor, she

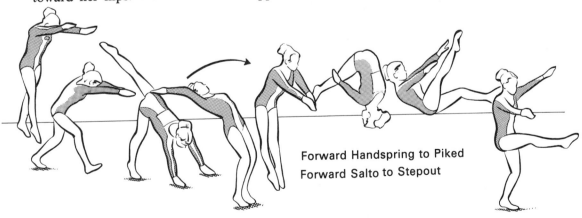

Forward Handspring to Piked
Forward Salto to Stepout

separates her legs and places one foot under her hips for the stepout landing.

If your forward handspring is strong enough, you may learn this skill in degrees by first performing tucked saltos without grasping your knees. Then, straighten your knees a little at a time, finally adding the stepout.

# FORWARD HANDSPRING TO LAYOUT FORWARD SALTO (VARIATION)

## Skill Level 8

See Forward Handspring (page 114), Forward Salto (page 134), and Forward Handspring to Tucked Forward Salto (page 139).

In this combination, the layout salto requires a very powerful forward handspring. The illustration shows a World Games finalist performing this combination in the floor-exercise event. As with the forward handspring to a piked salto, the performer lands the handspring in a slightly arched position in order to increase his range of motion for the ensuing pike. The degree of pike for the salto at takeoff always depends on the power of the handspring. After establishing initial rotation thrust, the performer extends his or her body to a straight or arched position. The arms are moved to the side to further shorten the radius of rotation.

Forward Handspring to Layout Forward Salto

# FORWARD HANDSPRING TO LAYOUT FORWARD SALTO STEPOUT (VARIATION)

## Skill Level 7

This technique may be learned by practicing a jump to a layout forward salto, with feet together, from a vaulting board into a crash mat. A strong run and a jump from the board should give you the elevation necessary to complete the rotation without stepping out. Eventually, add the stepout technique, which is similar to an aerial walkover.

## Spotting

See Forward Handspring to Tucked Forward Salto (page 139) for spotting hints.

Forward Handspring to Layout Forward Salto
to Stepout

# FORWARD HANDSPRING TO BARANI (VARIATION)

## Skill Level 7

Before attempting this combination, the performer should be able to execute a piked forward salto. The illustration shows an N.C.A.A. floor-exercise finalist performing. The series continued into a backward handspring to a backward salto combination.

Although it is imperceptible from the illustration, the performer twists slightly to the right as he leaves the mat for the jump. He then pulls his left arm downward, which shortens the left side of his body, encouraging further twist to the right. His right arm remains overhead in line with the long axis of his body. As the twist nears completion, his arms move slightly out to the side, which slows the twist, and toward the hips, which shortens the salto radius of rotation (speeds rotation). Considerable piking further increases the speed of salto rotation.

The landing position illustrated shows the tumbler coiled in readiness to continue backward into a handspring.

## Spotting

Spotting this skill is easy. Stand on the performer's left side as shown and place your right hand (forearm for heavy spot) on his or her stomach at takeoff. Reach across the back and grasp the waist on the far side. Guide the performer into the twist, salto, and landing.

Forward Handspring to Barani

# FORWARD HANDSPRING TO FORWARD SALTO WITH A FULL TWIST LEFT (VARIATION)

## Skill Level 9

This twisting salto skill requires knowing how to perform at least a partially laid-out forward salto. See Forward Handspring (page 114). Forward Salto (page 134), Forward Handspring to Tucked Forward Salto (page 139), and other similar combinations.

As the performer leaves the mat, she starts her twist. Her arms are held out away from the longitudinal axis of her body. She then pulls her arms close to her sides while simultaneously straightening her body for faster twisting rotation. Study the first four illustrations. You'll see that the performer could have watched the mat, if she wished, through most of the twist. But instead, she was probably more concerned with early visual recovery on the landing.

Although this performer didn't fall backward after she landed, her poor foot placement (well in front of her hips) and backward body tilt had to be compensated for by an excessive forward bend at the hips and knees.

This skill is best learned in an overhead twisting belt. Out of the belt, it may be learned as an extension of the barani or a pike forward salto with one-half twist. If you use the latter method, you will have no trouble orienting yourself for the direction of your second one-half twist. Twisting from a barani, though, does make optical orientation more difficult. If you perform the twist in your barani as you would in a "right-hand-down-first" roundoff, you will twist to the left and therefore your second one-half twist must also be executed to the left.

Forward Handspring to Forward Salto with a
Full Twist

**SIDE SALTO**

## Skill Level 6

The side salto may be learned by using the same basic "mat-pile" technique described for the forward salto earlier in the book (page 134).

    Biomechanically, this skill is a fairly efficient method for somersaulting. However, many performers become disoriented when rotating sideways. Generally, several repetitions on a trampoline, while using a safety belt, will solve this problem.

### Description

(1–3) Run and execute a skip step with a quarter turn to a two-foot landing. Jump and thrust arms (bent) upward with upper body leaning slightly in the direction of rotation. Watch the mat.

(4–6) Quickly, tuck with hands grasping area behind upper leg. If you keep your legs apart while you tuck, it will aid your rotation to some degree. Release your legs when the side of your body is approximately parallel to the floor, and step out.

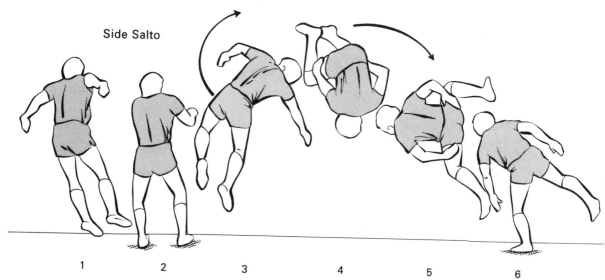

Side Salto

1    2    3    4    5    6

### Prerequisites

Cartwheel (page 102). Forward salto (page 134).

Spotting the Side Salto

## Spotting

See Cartwheel (page 102). Spot from the rear of the performer. Place your left hand on his or her waist (as shown in the illustration) at takeoff. Place your right hand on the other side. Support and guide performer throughout the skill.

# ROUNDOFF TO PIKED SIDE SALTO (VARIATION)

## Skill Level 7

This skill may be performed in a piked position or a straddled position. Learn to combine a roundoff (page 104) with a tucked side salto (page 146) before attempting to assume the piked position. Unlike the forward and backward

Roundoff to Piked Side Salto

salto, the piked position on a side salto is biomechanically more efficient than the tucked position. The side salto rotates on an anterior-posterior axis. Piking shortens the radius of rotation on that axis to a slightly greater degree than tucking does.

Roundoff to Tucked Double Side Salto

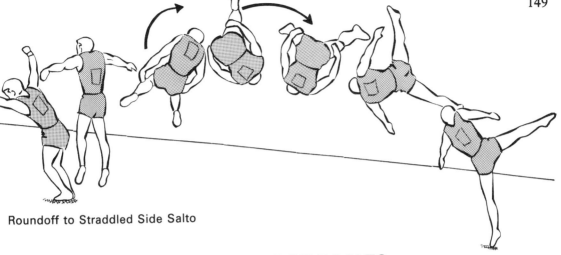

Roundoff to Straddled Side Salto

# ROUNDOFF TO TUCKED DOUBLE SIDE SALTO (VARIATION)

## Skill Level 10

This skill is rarely seen because it presents problems with orientation, spotting, and landing.

If you are the adventurous type and you want to demonstrate risk and originality in one skill, this may be the trick for you.

Because hand-spotting this maneuver is difficult, you had best learn it on a trampoline in a safety belt. Later transfer the skill to a foam rubber pit. Eventually, a mat should be placed over the foam pit to simulate regular landing conditions. The first few attempts on a regular matted area should involve a "catching mat," whereby four spotters lift the mat off the floor to soften the landing area. This is a standard spotting technique that can be used in practicing many skills in the gymnastics program.

## STANDING TUCKED BACKWARD SALTO

### Skill Level 6

Although this skill is generally taught after the performer has learned the backward handspring, many young gymnasts have the jumping power to learn it sooner. The weak jumper will find this skill very difficult unless it is preceded by a roundoff or backward handspring.

The body is airborne for a very brief period, so it must move quickly during the tucking and landing phases of the salto. Most coaches teach their gymnasts to grasp the lower leg, just below the knee, while doing the tuck. Other methods of tucking involve grasping the upper leg, just behind the knee joint (see illustration), or not grasping any portion of the body. The purpose of the grasp is to *insure* a tightly tucked position for fast rotation.

Standing Tucked Backward Salto

1  2  3  4  5

## Description

(1–3) Stand with arms held backward behind hips. Bend knees and jump with arms driving upward overhead. Be sure you *complete the jump* before bending your knees for the tuck. Tuck your hips under and press them upward as you jump. Do not place your head backward until the jump is completed.

(4–5) Quickly assume a tight tucked position using either method described earlier.

(6–7) Look for the mat as you release your tuck. Place your feet on the mat under your hips. Land with slightly bent hips and knees.

## Prerequisites

The ability to perform forward and backward handsprings is recommended. The ability to execute a fairly high vertical jump is essential.

## Spotting

(1–3) Stand at the performer's side. Place your left forearm under performer's lower back. Support and guide performer into the jump.

(4–5) Place your right hand on the back of performer's nearest thigh, and push upward to aid rotation.

(6–7) Quickly change hand positions to support the performer as he or she lands. Your left hand moves to the performer's lower back and your right hand supports the stomach area.

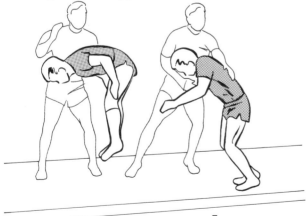

6         7

# STANDING BACKWARD HANDSPRING TO TUCKED BACKWARD SALTO DRILL

## Skill Level 6

### Description

(1–3) Execute a standing backward handspring with emphasis on leg push and fast arm thrust. Attempt to stay low and take a fair amount of distance. Concentrate on landing on your hands with your back arched, so you can snap down powerfully. Snap down to a high standing position with your arms extended forward.

(4–6) Jump upward leading with your arms (rather than head and shoulders). Note that the illustration shows a rather weak jump and poor arm thrust at takeoff. The performer's arms never get higher than shoulder level, the knees are bent a trifle early, and the head and shoulders lead the salto.

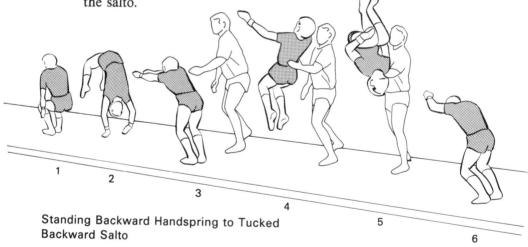

Standing Backward Handspring to Tucked
Backward Salto

### Prerequisites
Standing backward handspring. Standing tucked backward salto.

### Spotting
Stand to the side of the performer and spot the tucked salto. See Standing Tucked Backward Salto (page 150).

# ROUNDOFF TO BACKWARD HANDSPRING TO TUCKED BACKWARD SALTO

## Skill Level 6

Combining the roundoff and backward handspring into a salto requires some fast thinking from beginners who are often confused by the speed-timing relationship. The first two skills should be executed low and long for maximum push and linear speed. This action sets the performer up for maximum power in the final snapdown phase, which is essential for the jump.

1   2   3   4   5   6

Roundoff to Backward Handspring to Tucked Backward Salto

## Description

(1–3) Execute a roundoff to backward handspring. Snapdown with exaggerated force and with arms leading upward off the mat.

(4–6) Thrust arms upward *with the jump*. The hips should be pressed under (tight seat muscles) and should lead upward with the takeoff. The head should be held in a neutral position. Tuck tightly, then extend hips and knees for the landing. To absorb the shock of impact, always land with slightly bent hips and knees.

## Prerequisites

Roundoff to backward handspring (page 127). Standing tucked backward salto (page 150). Standing backward handspring to tucked backward salto (page 152) is recommended but not essential.

## Spotting

See Spotting for Backward Handspring (page 123).

# POORLY EXECUTED ROUNDOFF TO BACKWARD HANDSPRING TO TUCKED BACKWARD SALTO

## Skill Level 7

The following illustrations are presented as a model to show premature performance of the roundoff-to-backward-handspring-to-tucked-backward-salto series. The performer's snapdown action is so weak that it leaves her standing with her hands almost touching the mat. Her hips and knees are excessively bent. She is not able to rebound from snapdown to jump, so she must pause and lean backward to gain the proper balance for takeoff. The pause negates any power she might have received from the previous series of skills. However, because she knows she is being spotted, she attempts the backward salto.

Her lack of power from the snapdown, coupled with her desire to turn over, causes her to lean backward excessively without the benefit of arm thrust.

The spotter recognizes the problem and gives maximum support at takeoff, using both arms to guide and rotate the salto. The performer is literally lifted, rotated, and placed on her feet. Although the illustration demonstrates competent spotting, it also shows an overzealous beginner, foregoing proper learning progressions in pursuit of lofty goals.

In this case the coach and performer must recognize the performer's deficiencies in the preliminary setup skills (the roundoff and backward handspring). Repeating this poorly executed combination will never improve the salto. The coach and performer must *go back* and find the *root* of the problem, whether it be in the roundoff or the backward handspring, and master the essentials for quality performance.

Poorly Executed Roundoff to Backward Handspring
to Tucked Backward Salto

## Skill Level 7

The term "alternates" refers to a series that mixes saltos with backward handsprings. You should be able to perform a strong series of three or four backward handsprings to a tucked backward salto before attempting to learn this combination.

The first salto in this illustrated series is called a "whip back" because it is performed with a low and fast whipping action. It is executed in a similar manner as the backward handspring, but with added elevation and power. You must achieve a fair degree of hyperextension (arch) in your lower back with both arms thrusting backward, as if to place them on the mat. As you approach an inverted position, pike at the hips and allow your arms to move in front of your chest (both actions shorten the radius of rotation). Place your feet on the mat, under your hips and *watch the mat area in front of your feet.*

Continue backward into a backward handspring to salto. This series may be easily spotted by moving down the mat with the performer and supporting his or her lower back through each skill. I recommend the use of the overhead spotting belt.

Alternates

# WHIP-BACKWARD SALTO TO WHIP-BACKWARD SALTO (VARIATION)

## Skill Level 7

See description of Alternates. The whip-backward salto technique is used to build up or continue backward linear and rotary speed. The "whip back" may be substituted for a backward handspring, as a power base for twisting saltos, providing it *is* executed with power. Note though, the whip back is rarely used as a power base for multiple salto skills which require *maximum* efficiency at takeoff.

Compared with the backward handspring, a well-executed whip back is generally considered slightly less dynamic, and therefore somewhat more difficult to combine in a series.

Multiple whip backs in a series require that the performer place both feet under the hips (exact placement related to linear speed) upon landing in order to continue backward motion for the ensuing whip back. A powerful first whip back will obviously promote the performance of the second whip back, and so on.

Whip-backward Salto to Whip-backward Salto

# PIKED BACKWARD SALTO (VARIATION)

## Skill Level 6

This salto differs from most backward rotating skills in that the head is held forward for an extended period during takeoff. After the arms are thrust upward with the jump, they are moved downward toward the hips, simultaneously with the pike. Both movements create faster backward rotation because the length of the body is shortened substantially.

If the tumbler has initiated adequate thrust from the mat, the piked position may be "opened" to a laid-out position as the hips pass over the head. Further ahead in the section on twisting saltos, you will see how the opening from the pike provides an excellent vehicle for twisting.

Piked Backward Salto

# LAYOUT BACKWARD SALTO

## Skill Level 7

The layout backward salto action is *the* most important technique in advanced backward tumbling. The ability to rotate backward, with the body held straight, is the basis for most single-backward salto-twisting skills.

*Speed* must be established during the roundoff to backward handspring phase.

*Angle* is established as the result of a powerful snapdown, leaving the performer in perfect balance (in relation to his or her speed) for the jump.

*Timing* the jump and the arm thrust (simultaneous actions) is crucial for elevation and rotation. *Strength* is essential for fast reaction in conjunction with speed, angle, and timing.

Ideally, the layout backward salto should be executed with a straight body, because a slight arch or pike will retard subsequent twisting salto movements. However, the beginner may find the straight-body position somewhat inconsistent with "thrusting backward hard" into a layout salto. The natural tendency is to arch even when the hips are held tight. Arching is also biomechanically functional inasmuch as it shortens the radius of rotation to a small degree.

Once you've mastered the basic layout technique, you should try to maintain a straight body position throughout the salto.

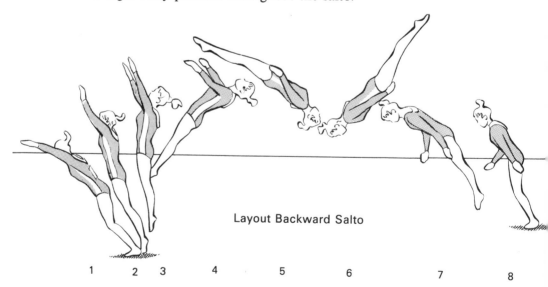

Layout Backward Salto

1    2    3    4    5    6    7    8

(1–3) Thrust arms backward quickly, toward the mat, on the handspring preceding the salto. Snapdown from the handstand with excessive force so you finish in a high standing position. Drive your arms upward, *directly from the mat,* into your jump. The ability to execute this action depends on the power of your snapdown. Press your hips upward and tighten your seat muscles as you leave the mat.

(4–8) Bring your arms down toward your hips. Maintain a tight hip position. As your body passes through the inverted position, look for the mat. Land with slightly bent hips and knees.

## Prerequisites

Roundoff to backward handspring to tucked backward salto. The ability to execute a whip-backward salto often proves helpful.

## Spotting

Place your hand on the performer's lower back and stomach after takeoff. Guide and support performer into the landing.

Spotting the Layout Backward Salto

# LAYOUT BACKWARD SALTO TO STEPOUT (VARIATION)

## Skill Level 6

The action of splitting the legs shortens the radius of rotation considerably, which makes this skill comparable in difficulty to a tucked backward salto. Notice also, the leg separation allows the performer to land with only three-quarters of the salto completed. This salto style is quite attractive and is often used as an interim technique, before a performer has mastered the layout salto with feet held together.

Discounting differences in elevation, this technique may be learned as an extension of a backward handspring to stepout. In this instance, the performer practices a high backward handspring until he or she is able to keep the hands from touching the mat. A little lower back support from a spotter will soon result in a low layout salto to a stepout.

Layout Backward Salto to Stepout

# BACKWARD SALTO WITH ONE-HALF TWIST (VARIATION)

## Skill Level 7

The twist in this skill is initiated either from the floor or in midair without support. In the former instance, the arms and shoulders lead slightly in the direction of the twist at the moment of the jump into the salto.

The illustration demonstrates the latter method of free-flight twisting, whereby the performer executes an arched layout salto with both arms driving symmetrically overhead. He then lowers his left arm faster than his right, which creates a small amount of twist toward the shorter side of his body (left side). Thereupon, he *straightens* his body with a twist of the hips to the left. As the motion of the hip twist slows, its momentum transfers to the entire body and completes the half turn. In effect, he is performing a "cat twist" in reverse. A falling cat twists off a modified piked position. The gymnast initiates his twist from a pike or an arch.

Generally, the most efficient method of twisting backwards utilizes the surface of support at takeoff.

## Spotting

Spot a left twist from the right side of the performer. Place your right hand under the performer's lower back at takeoff. As he or she approaches the inverted position, grasp the right hip with your left hand and assist the twist to the left. Support the landing.

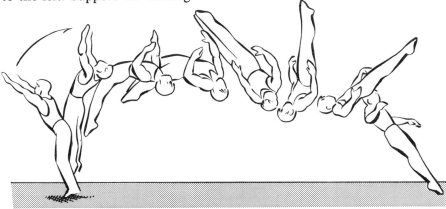

Backward Salto with One-half Twist

# BACKWARD SALTO WITH A FULL TWIST LEFT

## Skill Level 8

The most difficult obstacle facing the gymnast who performs this skill is initiating strong backward rotation while simultaneously establishing twist. In almost every instance, the beginner will overemphasize twisting at the expense of backward rotation. The result, even though the tumbler may have a perfectly fine layout salto, is an underrotated salto with a low squatty finish.

In order to complete a full-twisting salto, you need only twist about an eighth of a turn at takeoff. This limited twist easily allows the performer to concentrate on hip and arm thrust at takeoff. Unfortunately, due to the lack of facilities, many coaches must hand-spot this skill while teaching it, which often encourages twisting at the expense of backward rotation. The best teaching device remains the overhead spotting belt. Aside from its reliability, the overhead belt allows both performer and coach freedom of movement without compromise, unlike a hand spot.

## Description

(1–2) Execute a roundoff to a backward handspring. Snap down forcefully to a high standing position with arms thrusting overhead directly from the mat. Your arms should be held slightly wider than shoulders' width

Backward Salto with a Full Twist

apart. Jump upward with arms and shoulders executing about a one-eighth turn to the left. Tighten seat muscles and *press hips upward*. As your toes leave the mat, you must firmly establish your thrust for backward rotation.

(3–5) Look for the mat under your left armpit and pull arms in toward your chest. This arm action serves to speed up backward and twisting rotation simultaneously. Continue squeezing your hip muscles in order to maintain a straight body position. Watch the mat.

(6–8) As your body passes through an inverted position, move your arms away from your chest to slow the twist. Bend hips and knees slightly as you land.

If your goal is to tumble "through" the full twisting salto into a backward handspring, the salto should be executed at a lower level similar to a "whip back" described on page 156.

## Prerequisites
Roundoff to backward handspring to layout backward salto.

5          6          7          8

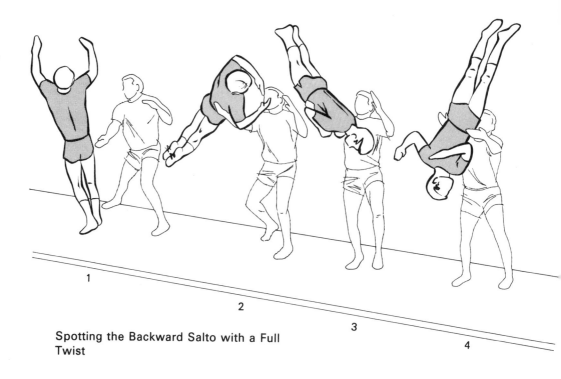

Spotting the Backward Salto with a Full
Twist

## Spotting

Hand-spot by standing on the right side of the performer, for a right twist.

(1–3) As the performer jumps upward and turns, place your right forearm under his or her stomach. The performer twists inward onto your extended right arm. Support and guide performer upward through an inverted position.

(4–6) Reach across performer's back with your left arm and grasp the right side of his or her hip. Pull right side of hip into the twist and continue supporting both sides of performer's body until he or she lands.

## THREE METHODS OF TEACHING THE BACKWARD SALTO WITH A FULL TWIST

There are three methods commonly being used to teach a full twisting backward salto. Each method involves starting the wrapping action for a full twist at a different time in the salto.

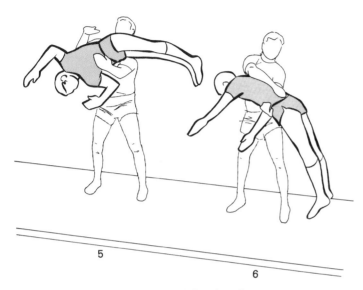

5

6

## The Early-Twisting Method

The *early-twisting method* is characterized by a starting action similar to the Arabian dive roll (see page 169), but with substantially more upward hip drive on takeoff. This method can be easily hand-spotted by a qualified coach. The performer executes a back dive one-half turn onto the extended arm of the spotter. The spotter then pulls the performer into an inverted position and twists the performer into the second half twist (as if spotting an aerial cartwheel). If you're strong enough to handle the performer safely, this is a good method of teaching the full twisting backward salto. And the hand spot is essential unless you have an overhead spotting belt or a tumbling pit.

## The Classical Method

The second method of teaching the full twisting backward salto is often termed the *classical method* because it simulates the best accepted method for performance. The early twist method often leaves the performer with very little hip drive into the salto. The classical method encourages hip drive to a much higher level before wrapping for the twist. This method is best taught in an overhead safety belt, although an extremely experienced spotter should be able to handle it.

The performer leaves the mat by thrusting the hips and arms upward and twisting the body about an eighth of a turn. As the hips pass through the horizontal, the performer pulls both arms close to the body (wrap) to speed up twisting, and the full twist is completed as the body passes through the inverted position. Both arms are extended out to the sides to slow the twist before the landing occurs.

## The Late-Twisting Method

The oldest method of performing the full twisting backward salto is the *late-twisting method*. The performer first learns a backward salto with one-half twist, the half twist is generally initiated by twisting the hips off an arched position and lowering the arm that corresponds to the direction of twist. The lowered arm is placed in line with the longitudinal axis of rotation, which speeds the twist to a small degree. Twisting and arm-lowering occur as the body passes through an inverted position. The late twist allows the performer to see the landing area before executing the first half twist. The performer then attaches the last half twist onto the first, generally performing it by "feel" rather than by sight. As this technique is mastered, most performers start twisting earlier for more efficiency. Many coaches teach this method to beginners who have difficulty combining hip drive with twisting on the takeoff. It allows the beginner to concentrate on hip drive first and twisting second. Although this method is not biomechanically efficient, it has a place in certain problem situations.

# PIKED BACKWARD SALTO WITH FULL TWIST RIGHT (VARIATION)

## Skill Level 8

See Piked Backward Salto (page 157). This skill involves twisting in free flight and without the aid of the support surface. The general pattern of this skill is best learned wearing a spotting belt on the trampoline, whereby the beginning performer has enough time to assume the various body positions.

The head should be held forward during the piking phase in order to establish a point of orientation. When your upper back is approximately parallel to the floor, forcefully extend your hips and turn your upper body in the direction of the twist. Bring your arms close to your chest and look for the landing area.

Piked Backward Salto with a Full Twist

# BACKWARD SALTO WITH DOUBLE TWIST

## Skill Level 9

Once you have mastered the backward salto with a double twist, a full twisting salto feels like a mere floating turn in the air. You can experience the difference by performing each of the twists from an erect standing position.

There are subtle differences that characterize both skills, in regard to body position at takeoff. Because these twists are initiated from the floor, the jump into a double twist shows a wider arm position and more upper-torso turn than

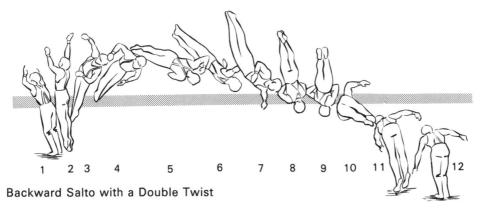

1  2  3    4      5      6    7    8   9   10  11      12

Backward Salto with a Double Twist

the full twisting salto. These twisting takeoff positions are indicative of "twisting potential." Once the position for twisting potential has been established, the performer wraps his or her arms inward toward the long axis of the body, as quickly as possible.

### Description

(1–2)   Execute a roundoff to backward handspring. Snap down from the handspring to a standing position with arms driving upward directly from the mat. Your arms should be held significantly wider than shoulders' width apart as they thrust backward and into the twist. Squeeze your seat muscles and *press your hips upward.*

(3–12)  Quickly wrap the twist by pulling your left elbow in toward your side and throwing your right arm downward across and into your chest. The force and direction of the wrapping action usually create a slight bend in the performer's hips. Although many performers can watch the mat from "wrap" to finish, most tumblers rely on kinesthetic awareness to land with control. Extend your arms out to the side to slow the twist for landing. Always land with slightly bent hips and knees.

### Prerequisites
Roundoff to Backward Handspring (page 127) to Backward Salto with a Full Twist (page 162).

### Spotting
I recommend using the trampoline as a starting place for learning this skill. Then practice it further in an overhead twisting belt or as an extension of a full twist into a foam rubber pit.

## BACKWARD SALTO WITH A TRIPLE TWIST (VARIATION)

## Skill Level 10

This skill was first introduced in world-class floor-exercise competition by a male Japanese Olympian named Eizo Kenmotsu, in 1970. Needless to say, Eizo spun very fast and went rather high. The illustration shows his performance which is characterized by the tightness of his wrap throughout all three twists.

## ARABIAN DIVE ROLL

### Skill Level 5

The term "Arabian" is used because a group of world-famous Moroccan circus tumblers (circa 1930), performing the half twist to a forward salto in their act, wore Bedouin costumes suggesting Arabian origins. Americans use the term "Arabian" to describe a jump with one-half turn into any forward-rotating skill.

The Arabian jumping technique is popular among tumblers because it allows them to reap the benefits of a powerful backward snapdown prior to executing a standard forward rotating skill. Many tumblers use it instead of a forward handspring as a vehicle for projecting into forward saltos, walkovers, and dive rolls.

## Description

(1–3) Execute a roundoff, or roundoff to backward handspring. Land on your feet in a fairly high standing position with slightly bent hips and knees.

Jump upward with arms driving overhead (slightly wider than shoulders' width apart). As the jump occurs, the arms and shoulders make about an eighth turn in the direction of the twist. Squeeze your seat muscles and stretch.

When performing Arabian and backward salto skills, always concentrate on driving your hips (center of gravity) upward as you jump. When twisting, add a turn of the hips in the direction of the twist. Hip turn, shoulder turn, and arm width at takeoff all indicate the degree of "potential twist." Thus, a multiple twist shows more hip turn, shoulder turn, and a wider arm position at takeoff than a half twist. After establishing potential twisting thrust by pushing off the mat, the performer "wraps" by bringing both arms quickly inward, toward the long axis of his or her body.

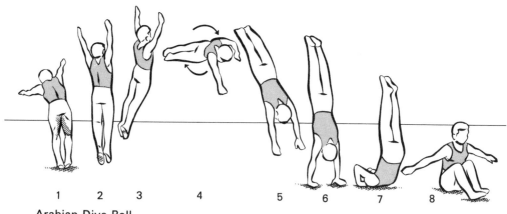

1   2   3   4   5   6   7   8

Arabian Dive Roll

(4–6) Look for the mat and hold a tight hip position. Many performers prefer to arch at the highest point of the jump, which creates a "stalling effect." You may find the arched position aesthetically more appealing than the austere straight body position. Both attitudes are technically acceptable.

As your body approaches the inverted position, stretch your shoulders and reach for the mat. Bend your elbows as your hands touch the mat and watch the mat between your hands.

(7–8) Lower the back of your head and shoulders to the mat as you bend at the hips. Bend your knees and roll forward to a stand.

## Prerequisites

Straight body dive roll. Arabian dive to forward roll from a stand. Strong roundoff or backward handspring.

Spotting the Arabian Dive Roll

## Spotting

The performer should learn the basic Arabian action from a standing position on very soft mats. The spotting technique is essentially the same from a stand or a run. You may spot from either side of the performer. The illustration shows the performer twisting away from the spotter. In this case, the spotter supports and twists the performer at takeoff, and spots the landing by reaching across the performer's back and grasping his or her hip.

If you wish the performer to twist into you, have him or her jump with a half turn and roll onto your near arm (your left arm for a left twist). Now you are supporting his or her stomach with your forearm. Grasp the side of the near hip with your other hand, and guide the performer into the forward roll.

## ARABIAN DIVE TO FULL TWIST AND ROLL (VARIATION)

### Skill Level 8

### Description

(1–2) Try to land in a high standing position from the previous skill so your arms may be thrown overhead without hesitation. Jump with body and arms turning toward the right. Watch the mat in front of you and then around the side as your body half turns. Arms should be held wider than shoulders' width apart in preparation for the ensuing wrap into the twist. Look for the mat under your right arm as you execute the half turn.

(3–4) To wrap the twist, bring right arm over your head in line with the vertical axis of rotation and simultaneously wrap your left arm across your chest.

(5–7) Turn your head in the direction of the twist and reach for the mat as your body passes through a horizontal position. Look for the landing area.

(8–9) Bend elbows and guide upper back to the mat. Roll forward to feet.

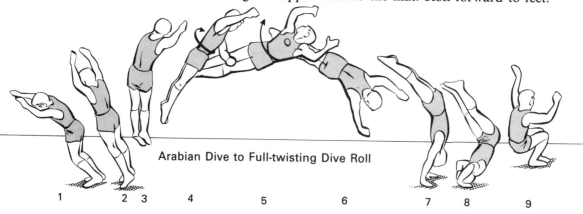

Arabian Dive to Full-twisting Dive Roll

1    2    3    4    5    6    7    8    9

## Prerequisites

Roundoff or backward handspring to back-dive, one-half twist to forward roll, and full-twisting dive roll.

Spotting the Arabian Dive to Full-twisting
Dive Roll

## Spotting

This skill is best learned in an overhead safety belt. If the overhead belt is not available, use a tumbling pit or crash mats for the landing area. See Full-twisting Dive Roll (page 94) for an additional mat-spotting technique.

This roll may be hand-spotted by an advanced spotter. In this case, the performer twists into the spotter, who grasps the performer just prior to landing and guides the roll (see illustration).

# ARABIAN DIVE TO TUCKED FORWARD SALTO TO STEPOUT

## Skill Level 6

### Description

(1–2) Execute a roundoff, or roundoff to backward handspring. Snap down to a high landing position with arms driving upward overhead. Tilt hips upward in the direction of the twist as you jump. Simultaneously, turn your arms and shoulders in the direction of the twist.

(3–4) Look for the mat as your body turns one quarter. Pull your arms toward your hips (you may grasp your knees), and tuck your knees up to your stomach. Simultaneously, duck your chin in toward your chest and round your back.

(5–6) When your back is approximately parallel to the mat, extend your hips and legs for the stepout. Look forward, past your legs, for optical orientation. Place your first landing foot under your hips, and step out.

### Prerequisites
Arabian dive roll. Forward salto to stepout.

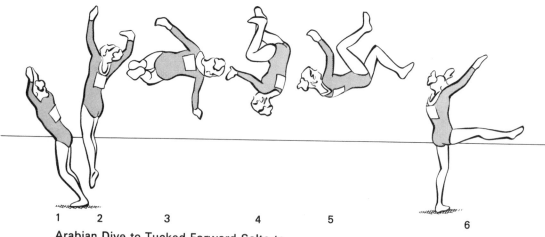

Arabian Dive to Tucked Forward Salto to Stepout

## Spotting

This skill is best learned in an overhead spotting belt. To hand-spot, stand on the side of the performer in the direction he or she will twist.

(1–3) As the performer leaves the mat, reach under the lower back and allow him or her to roll the half twist onto your forearm. The performer's stomach is now resting on your forearm.

(4–6) Reach across the back with your other arm and support the lower back as he or she turns over. Support performer right up to the landing.

# ARABIAN DIVE TO PIKED FORWARD SALTO (VARIATION)

## Skill Level 6

At the instant of takeoff, the piked salto requires a more forceful jump and hip thrust upward than a tucked Arabian salto requires. The speed and depth of the pike will help accelerate rotation. Over a period of time, you may learn to assume the piked position by simply tucking your tucked Arabian salto less.

Arabian Dive to Piked Forward Salto

# ARABIAN DIVE TO PIKED FORWARD SALTO TO STEPOUT (VARIATION)

## Skill Level 7

Once a piked salto is learned, the stepout modification is relatively easy to incorporate. In the early stages, a slight leg split upon landing simply progresses to a more substantial one. As the performer develops more confidence, the leg split is initiated earlier in the salto.

Arabian Dive to Piked Forward Salto to Stepout

# ARABIAN DIVE TO LAYOUT FORWARD SALTO TO STEPOUT (VARIATION)

## Skill Level 7

This salto technique requires more rotational power at takeoff than a tucked salto does. The performer drives both arms overhead, into the twist, as he or she jumps. *Upward hip thrust* must also be firmly established at takeoff. The performer does a leg split and moves both arms out to the sides of the body.

The leg split and the arm placement serve to accelerate forward rotation. The sideward arm placement also slows the initial twist that was created at takeoff because the arms are extended away from the body's twisting axis.

The performer's body follows the basic pattern of an aerial walkover to a stepout. See Arabian Dive to Tucked Forward Salto (page 174) for spotting techniques.

Arabian Dive to Layout Forward Salto to
Stepout

# ARABIAN DIVE TO TUCKED FORWARD ONE-AND-ONE-QUARTER SALTO (VARIATION)

## Skill Level 7

Any skill that requires rotation beyond one salto demands the full respect of coach and performer. Before attempting such skills, the performer should develop a high degree of kinesthetic awareness through repetition under safe conditions.

This skill may be learned as an extension of the Arabian Dive to Tucked Forward Salto (page 174). The performer must practice, *by degrees,* overrotating the normal tucked salto into a crash mat.

As this skill is perfected, the arms become the main means of support on the landing. A smooth, strong bending of the arms absorbs the shock of landing until the feet touch and safely *spread* the impact through the length of the body.

Arabian Dive to Tucked One-and-one-quarter Salto

## ARABIAN DIVE TO TUCKED FORWARD ONE-AND-ONE-HALF SALTO (VARIATION)

### Skill Level 9

This skill should be learned in an overhead safety belt or with a foam pit. If the safety belt is used, the spotter must be very experienced because of the hands-first landing the skill requires. The performer must be 100 percent successful performing the skill in the belt before trying it unaided. A very soft landing mat should be used at every training session.

Before attempting to learn this skill, the performer should be capable of executing an Arabian dive to piked forward salto. The initial power thrust at takeoff is approximately similar for both skills.

Arabian Dive to Tucked One-and-one-half
Salto

## TUCKED DOUBLE BACKWARD SALTO

### Skill Level 9

This skill was first introduced in national-level competition in the early 1950s by a tumbling specialist named Richard Browning. During the same period, the first female tumbler noted for this skill was Jo Ann Mathews. Both tumblers received their early training at the Dallas Athletic Club in Texas. In 1959, Jamile Ashmore won the national floor exercise title using this skill on a hardwood floor.

If you can execute a layout backward salto to a landing on your back (one-and-one-quarter salto), you are capable of generating enough power to turn over twice in a tucked position.

The power thrust (for rotation and elevation at takeoff) must be *substantial.* You must not allow your eagerness to assume a tucked position interfere

180

with your initial thrust for rotation. You may grasp your lower leg, just below the knee, or grasp the back of your upper leg (as illustration shows) when tucking. Although it is not aesthetically appealing, you may also spread your knees to speed rotation.

## Description

(1–3) Execute a roundoff to a backward handspring. Snap down to a high standing position with your arms thrusting overhead directly from the mat. *A powerful arm and upper-body thrust is essential.* Jump with arms driving upward and backward. Hold head forward until you start to tuck.

(4–9) Quickly bring your arms downward and grasp your legs in a tight, tucked position. Try to orient yourself visually as you complete the first salto. Look for the landing area as you release your tuck. Land with your feet under your hips. Note that the tightness of the tuck tends to increase until the leg release occurs.

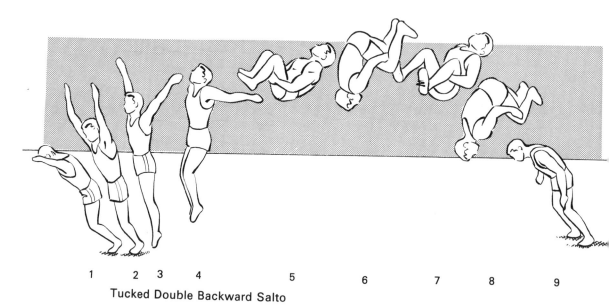

| 1 | 2 | 3 | 4 | 5 | 6 | 7 | 8 | 9 |

Tucked Double Backward Salto

## Prerequisites

A high tucked backward salto with an early opening (see illustration). Ability to overrotate a layout backward salto to a back landing on crash mats.

High Tucked Backward Salto with Early
Opening

## Spotting

Learn this skill in an overhead safety belt. See suggested progressions for
learning Backward One-and-one-half Salto with One-and-one-half Twist (pages
186–187).

As the takeoff occurs, the spotter may aid rotation by quickly boosting the
performer's hips from the rear. The spotter should then follow the performer's
pattern of rotation. As the performer turns the last salto, the spotter may reach
under his or her back and partially support the landing.

# PIKED DOUBLE BACKWARD SALTO (VARIATION)

## Skill Level 9

See Tucked Double Backward Salto (page 179).

This skill is an obvious extension of the tucked double salto; however, the
piked position requires more initial thrust at takeoff. The head is generally held
forward for a longer period as the body rises, in order to insure an efficient
piking action.

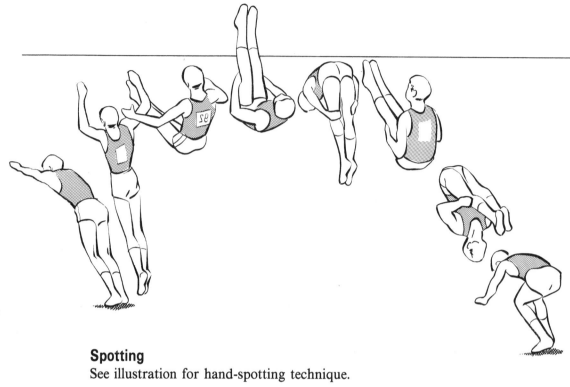

## Spotting
See illustration for hand-spotting technique.

Hand Push for Double Salto

# LAYOUT DOUBLE BACKWARD SALTO (VARIATION)

## Skill Level 10

This skill was first exhibited in 1978 world-class competition by a Russian gold-medal winner named Nikolai Andrianov.

Turning over twice in a layout position requires more initial thrust at takeoff than does any other type of double salto. After the jump, the arms are lowered and the back is arched to speed rotation. Although not aesthetically desirable, the illustrated performance shows slightly bent knees and a pronounced pike-down for the landing, which act to shorten the body and speed rotation. See Tucked Double Backward Salto (page 179) for additional information.

Layout Double Backward Salto

# FULL-TWISTING DOUBLE-BACKWARD SALTO

## Skill Level 10

Any double salto with a twist is called a "Fliffis." The slang term for this particular Fliffis is "Full in—Back out," which means the first salto is a full-twisting backward one, and the second is straight backward. Other common full-twisting double salto combinations are "Half in—Half out" and "Back in —Full out." In the 1980 N.C.A.A. floor exercise finals, Steve Eliot performed a "Full in—Full out Fliffis."

The power thrust necessary at takeoff for this skill is similar to the thrust required for a piked double-backward salto. The full twist is performed in a "puck" (open tuck) position and is completed by the apex of the jump. This gives the performer the time necessary to complete the second salto. Most performers tuck with an under-the-thigh grasp for the second salto, in order to avoid missing their knees with their hands. Weaker performers can also increase salto rotation by holding their legs wider apart.

Full-twisting Double-backward Salto (weak version)

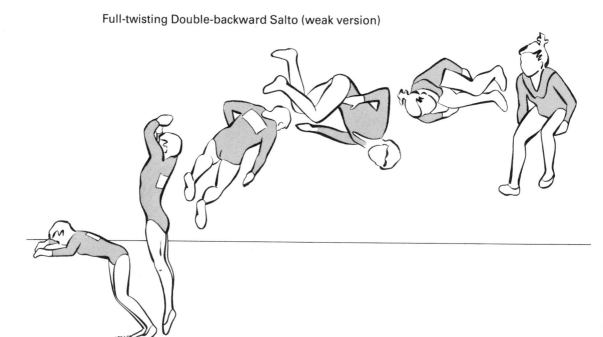

Full-twisting Double-backward Salto (strong version)

Learn this skill on a trampoline in an overhead spotting belt. You may watch the mat during the full-twisting salto to gain orientation. As the full twist nears completion, pull your knees upward into a tuck by grasping the back of your thighs. (Many performers practice overrotating the full twist to a back drop landing until they feel the confidence to turn over the second salto.) Hold your knees wide to facilitate backward rotation and slow the twist. The change of body shape from puck to tuck will also retard the speed of the twist. Unless you are extremely high in the air, you will not be able to see the landing area until a moment before landing.

Transfer this technique to the tumbling mats in an overhead safety belt. It is wise to use a crash mat on the landing area so you can get used to measuring your steps for future inground pit practice. After you have mastered the skill on the mats in the belt, you are ready to try it out of the belt and into a foam rubber pit. Once this proves successful, place a mat over the pit and practice landing on a relatively firm surface.

## BACKWARD ONE-AND-ONE-HALF SALTO WITH ONE-AND-ONE-HALF TWIST (VARIATION)

### Skill Level 10

This apparently complicated skill was performed for the first time in world championship competition in 1979 by a gold-medal winner named Kurt Thomas.

Backward One-and-one-half Salto with
One-and-one-half Twist

The semi-tucked position demonstrated throughout the performance is called a "puck," which, like the tuck, accelerates backward rotation considerably. Twisting, however, is difficult in the puck because the knees are extended away from the vertical axis of the body.

The performer must learn to oversomersault the full-twisting backward salto, look over the shoulder for an additional one-half twist, and continue into a forward roll. The prerequisites for this skill should include: (1) a tucked double backward salto, (2) an Arabian dive to full twist to forward roll, (3) a backward salto with a full twist, and (4) an Arabian dive to tucked forward one-and-one-half salto.

Learn this skill on a trampoline in an overhead spotting belt. Execute an overrotated backward salto with a full twist. Look over your shoulder in the same direction as the twist and reach for the trampoline. Your spotter should support your hands-first landing. After this trampoline technique is perfected, use a tumbling mat and safety belt and practice the same sequence from a roundoff backward handspring. Your first attempts out of the belt should be executed into a foam rubber pit. Once this proves successful, place a mat over the pit so you can practice rolling on a relatively firm surface.

## DOUBLE-TWISTING DOUBLE-BACKWARD SALTO

### Skill Level 10

This skill was first demonstrated in national collegiate championship competition by Steve Elliot in 1980. My illustration shows the performance of a Chinese national gymnastics team member in 1981.

1    2    3    4

**Double-twisting Double-backward Salto**

10          11                    12                    13

14

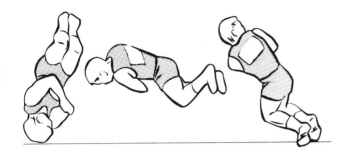

7         8         9

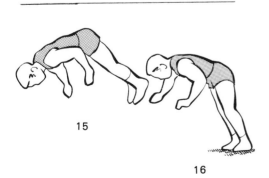

15

16

I strongly recommend learning this skill by using a trampoline and safety belt before attempting it on the floor. Once the trampoline technique has been mastered, the next step should involve many weeks of training on a floor mat in a safety belt. If the performer can execute this skill consistently on the floor, the third step should be carried out with the use of a foam-rubber landing pit. Once this step proves successful, a landing mat is then placed over the pit to simulate landing conditions on a flat surface.

The prerequisite skills are a full-twisting double-backward salto (page 184) and a double-twisting backward salto (page 167).

Note that the performer's center of gravity is at its peak during the completion of the first full twist (fig. 8). This position also affords a brief moment of optical orientation with the landing surface. The head continues turning and optical orientation is again achieved as a full and one-half twist nears completion (fig. 14). Prior to the landing (fig. 15), the mat is once again in view as the arms are extended away from the body to slow the twist.

# Glossary

Aerial Skills: A 360-degree somersault initiated from one foot to a one- or two-foot landing.

Alternates: Somersaults performed alternately with backward handsprings in a series.

Arabian Dive: A jump with a half twist into a forward roll or forward somersault.

Arch: A basic position in which the back is hyper-extended (curved backward) while the hips and knees are held straight.

Barani (Baroni): A forward somersault with one half twist whereby the performer watches the mat throughout the movement.

Block: The process of forcefully pushing against the surface of support with the arms (hands) or legs (feet) in a direction that is opposite the established flow of motion in order to elevate the body.

Center of Gravity: The point in the body which represents the center of the mass.

Crash Mat: A large, soft mat made with foam rubber used to absorb the impact of landing.

Extension: The process of decreasing the angle in joint areas. Complete extension is achieved when the joint is straight.

Flexion: The process of increasing the angle in joint areas. Complete flexion is achieved when the joint is bent maximally.

Fliffis: Any double somersault with a twist.

Hurdle: The process of leaping, while moving forward, from one foot to both feet or from one foot to a landing on the same foot (Skip-step Hurdle). The hurdle allows the performer to maintain forward running speed while changing leg position for projection into the ensuing skill.

Inverted: A vertical position with the body held upside down, as in a handstand.

Layout: A straight-body or slightly arched-body position.

Linear Motion: Movement in one direction without deviation.

Pike: The hips are bent, to varying degrees, with the knees held straight.

Rebound: A spring back (bounce) from the force of landing on the arms or legs.

Roll: A rotating skill that is characterized by contact with the back on the mat.

Salto (Somersault): A complete rotation of the body (360°) from feet to feet unless more rotation is specified, as in a double salto.

Shoot: The process of extending the hips, with the legs leading, in order to give the body impetus in a given direction.

Skip-step Hurdle: A step-hop-step movement that is used prior to the performance of a handspring and other "kick over" tumbling skills.

Snapdown (Mule Kick): A movement that is initiated from a handstand position and finishes on flat feet as a result of a quick hip flexion accompanied with an arm push and shoulder extension.

Spotting: Refers to the system of manually assisting or being ready to manually assist the performer.

Stepout: The process of placing one foot in front of the other during the final phase of a skill in order to continue moving into a skill that requires a one-foot take-off.

Tuck: Maximum bending of the hips and knees with the back rounded forward.

Twist: Often used interchangeably with "turn." A rotation right or left around the vertical axis of the body.

Whip back: A fast, low, backward somersault that closely resembles a backward handspring. This style of somersault is used to increase difficulty while at the same time maintaining linear speed.